Photography: An Independent Art

Photography: An Independent Art

Photographs from the Victoria and Albert Museum 1839-1996

Mark Haworth-Booth

V&A Publications

First published by V&A Publications, 1997

V&A Publications
160 Brompton Road
London SW3 1HW

ISBN: 1 85177 204 9

A catalogue record for this book is available from the British Library

Designed by Tim Harvey

Originated by Colorlito Rigogliosi srl, Milan

Printed in Singapore by C.S. Graphics

Front cover: Herbert Bayer (1900–85), *Metamorphosis*, 1936
Back cover: Frederick Hollyer (1837–1933), *Mrs Patrick Campbell*, 1893

Frontispiece: William Wegman (American, b.1943), *Dressed for Ball*, 1988. Polacolor II. 20 × 24 inches (61.0 × 50.8 cm). Bought 1988. E.858 1989

Contents

Introduction 8

CHAPTER ONE
The New Art 11

CHAPTER TWO
A Vibrant Populist Enterprise 35

CHAPTER THREE
All the World under the Subjugation of Art 55

CHAPTER FOUR
A Fine Art and a Manufacturing Art 73

CHAPTER FIVE
The Cosmopolitan Archive 101

CHAPTER SIX
Being Contemporary 129

CHAPTER SEVEN
The National Collection of the Art of Photography 153

CHAPTER EIGHT
Fond Wrestlers with Photography 181

Abbreviations and Notes 203

Index 206

Photographic acknowledgements and credits

We are grateful to the many photographers represented in the V&A collection who kindly sign an agreement allowing their works to be illustrated in the Museum's publications and educational programmes, and to be used also in publicity for the Museum's activities. Their generosity is greatly appreciated. We are also most grateful to the agencies, estates and individuals who have given their permission for the illustration of works in this publication, and to the colleagues who have helped us to identify copyright holders.

In particular, we should like to record the Museum's gratitude for the use of work by the following: Herbert Bayer, with thanks to Mrs Herbert Bayer, Mr Javan Bayer and Mr Jonathan Bayer; Cecil Beaton, by courtesy of the Cecil Beaton archive at Sotheby's, with thanks to Philippe Garner and Lydia Cresswell-Jones; Richard Billingham, by courtesy of Anthony Reynolds Gallery, London; Bill Brandt © Bill Brandt Archive Ltd., with thanks to John-Paul Kernot; Marcel Broodthaers, by kind courtesy of Maria Gilissen; Henri Cartier-Bresson, by courtesy of Magnum Photos, with thanks to Henri Cartier-Bresson; Helen Chadwick, by courtesy of the Estate of Helen Chadwick, with thanks to David Notarius (installation photographs by Edward Woodman); Hugo Erfurth, by kind courtesy of Marianne Erfurth; Walker Evans, © Walker Evans Archive, The Metropolitan Museum of Art, New York; Rotimi Fani-Kayode, by courtesy of Autograph, the Association of Black Photographers, London, with thanks to Mark Sealy; Masahisa Fukase, by courtesy of Masahisa Fukase Estate, with thanks to Koko Yamagishi; David Hockney, © David Hockney (photograph: Steve Oliver), with thanks to Karen Kuhlman; E.O. Hoppé, © The E.O. Hoppé Trust, Curatorial Assistance Inc., Los Angeles, with thanks to Graham Howe; George Hoyningen-Huene, copyright of Horst P. Horst, New York, with thanks also to Hamiltons Gallery, London and *Vogue*, Paris; Ida Kar, by courtesy of Mary Evans Picture Library; Annette Lemieux, by courtesy of David McKee Gallery, New York; Lee Miller, © Lee Miller Archive, with thanks to Antony Penrose; Laszlo Moholy-Nagy, by kind courtesy of Hattula Moholy-Nagy; Raymond Moore, by courtesy of Mary Cooper; Gabriel Orozco, by courtesy of Marian Goodman Gallery, New York; Irving Penn, *Harlequin Dress (Lisa Fonssagrives-Penn, New York*, 1950, is ©, copyright renewed 1978, by Condé Nast Publications Inc., New York and appears with special thanks to Irving Penn; Man Ray, © Man Ray Trust/ADAGP, Paris and DACS, London 1997; Edward Steichen, by courtesy of Steichen Carousel, New York, with thanks to Joanna T. Steichen and Laurie Platt Winfrey; Joel Sternfeld, © Joel Sternfeld, by courtesy of PaceWildensteinMacGill, New York, with thanks to Peter MacGill and Laura Santaniello; Paul Strand, © 1983 Aperture Foundation, Inc., Paul Strand Archive, by courtesy of the Paul Strand Archive of Aperture Foundation, with thanks to Michael E. Hoffman; William Wegman, © William Wegman, by courtesy of PaceWildensteinMacGill, New York, with thanks to Bridget Shields, William Wegman Studio.

Because of their vintage, many of the original prints copied for this book show surface marks and silver sublimation which can – when copied – obscure the image. In order to compensate for this the prints were photographed using cross-polarised light. This reduces scattered light from the surface and allows the viewer to see the image more clearly. The film used to make the copy images was Fuji 5×4 inch 64T film. The author and James Stevenson, Manager of the V&A Photographic Studio, thank Fuji UK Ltd, and especially Trevor Drake, for their kind support in supplying, free of charge, the film used in making the copies for this book.

MH-B

Acknowledgements

Many individuals have very kindly helped to bring this book to completion, and I am most grateful to all of them. The expertise and enthusiasm of Michael Conforti, Director of the Sterling and Francine Clark Art Institute, Williamstown, Massachusetts, gave the idea for the book impetus in its earliest stages. It was written during a three-month secondment to the V&A's Research Department in 1996 and I greatly benefited from seminars and conversations involving many colleagues, in particular Paul Greenhalgh, Head of Research, Malcolm Baker, Deputy Head of Research and Dr Clive Wainwright. The Museum's Registry and Archive of Art and Design traced many obscure records and Helen Pye-Smith of the National Art Library brought the Cameron letters to my attention. I was given invaluable help by Virginia Dodier of the Department of Photography at The Museum of Modern Art, New York and Divia Patel in the V&A's Indian and South East Asian Department. While any faults of emphasis or exclusion in the selection of images for the book are, of course, entirely my own, I should like to acknowledge the ideas generously offered by Mark Holborn, editor at Jonathan Cape, Graham Howe, Director of Curatorial Assistance, Inc., and Weston Naef, Curator of Photographs at the J. Paul Getty Museum. For their comments on the text, I am grateful to Michael Conforti, Susan Lambert, Chief Curator of Prints, Drawings and Paintings, and Timothy Stevens, Assistant Director (Collections). My warm thanks also to James Stevenson, Head of Photography, and my editor Tim Ayers. Warm thanks are also due to my colleagues in the Department of Textiles and Dress, Valerie Mendes and Amy de le Haye for help on fashion, and Linda Parry for advice on the arts and crafts movement. I am also grateful to Professor Joel Snyder of the University of Chicago for sharing his knowledge on many subjects and occasions. For commissioning articles that have helped me focus on some of the topics developed in this book, I thank the editors, past and present, of *Aperture*, the *British Journal of Photography*, *Creative Camera*, *History of Photography* and *The Times Literary Supplement*. I also want to pay tribute to my late friend Sir Tom Hopkinson, distinguished editor of *Picture Post*. Tom asked me – fifteen years ago – to write an article about the dramatic change in the status of photography in the 1970s and early 1980s. At the time I thought the whole thing was self-evident and so I didn't write the piece. I realized later that the fluctuations in status and role have the much longer – and, I think, more interesting – history recounted here.

The V&A's collection of the art of photography has been built up and cared for by many hands, known and unknown, over the generations from 1856 to 1996. I should like to thank with especial gratitude all the colleagues who have worked closely with me during the last twenty years: David Wright (1977–9), Alexandra Noble (1979–84), Christopher Titterington (1984–95), Sarah Postgate (1987–92), Catherine Bindman (1992–3), Charlotte Cotton (from 1993) and Martin Barnes (from 1996). The book is dedicated to everyone whose gifts – of all kinds – have enhanced the V&A Photography Collection.

Introduction

This is a book about the art of photography. It is the first introduction to the Victoria and Albert Museum's Photography Collection, which is international and ranges from 1839 to the present day. We hope that the book will give a vivid idea of the quality and diversity of the Museum's holdings. One hundred images have been selected from a total of some 300,000.

Photography has been actively exhibited and collected by many art museums in the last 20-25 years. Before that, there was the bright but lonely beacon of the Department of Photography at The Museum of Modern Art, New York, founded in 1940. Yet further back, there had been talented curator-collectors, such as Dr Carl Glaser, Director of the Kunstbibliothek in Berlin. His inspired acquisitions of avant-garde photography came suddenly to an end – because he was Jewish – in 1933.[1] There is a large history to be written about the ways in which the art of photography has been collected and understood by museums and related institutions. One of the longest perspectives – and perhaps one of the most illuminating – is provided by the Photography Collection at the Victoria and Albert Museum.

The V&A grew out of the South Kensington Museum, which was founded in 1856. Henry Cole, the first Director, began the collection of the art of photography in the same year. Simultaneously Cole took up photography himself, as an amateur, and established a photographic service to copy works of art for educational purposes. Soldiers trained in photography at the South Kensington Museum photographed on expeditions to remote lands. As the Museum achieved global renown, its Photography Collection became a world resource. However, the Museum was also the first to buy and exhibit the radical photographs of Julia Margaret Cameron in 1865, and it received one of the finest early private collections of photography by bequest in 1868. No other museum in the world – whether in Berlin, Paris or New York – did so much with photography or collected so well.

However, the narrative of photography and its shifting status as an art is full of twists and turns. The complexities are exemplified in the tale told here. This is also the story of photography's evolution from art to industry, and into a medium which could, of course, be both. This was recognized by the Commissioners of the International Exhibition held in South Kensington in 1862, who decided, after much deliberation, that photography should be classified as 'an independent art'. By the twentieth century photographs were essential social facts, and began to be distributed everywhere, overwhelmingly, in magazines and books. The Museum started collecting classic early photography, retrospectively, in the 1930s and contemporary photographic art once more from 1964. In 1977 the V&A became responsible for the 'national collection of the art of photography in the United Kingdom'. A period of systematic collecting began. The book concludes with a selection of international photographs mostly acquired in 1996, 140 years after Cole began the world's earliest collection of the art of photography.

Like all great museums, the V&A has many collections of photographs. The V&A's Theatre Museum, for example, has its own rich archive, as has the Indian and South East Asian Department. This book draws only on the Photography Collection in the Department of Prints, Drawings and Paintings, plus some essential items from the National Art Library, which holds important publications such as Talbot's *The Pencil of Nature* (1844–6). Technical data have been kept to a minimum, as the Museum's *A Guide to Early Photographic Processes* by Brian Coe and the present writer (V&A, 1983) is still in print.

I was able to draw on a valuable new history of the V&A: *A Grand Design: The Art of the Victoria and Albert Museum*, edited by Malcolm Baker and Brenda Richardson, was published in 1997.[2] A checklist of all the exhibitions held at the Museum, including photographic shows, is also newly available, compiled by Elizabeth James.[3]

Finally, this publication celebrates the opening of a new photography gallery at the Victoria and Albert Museum in which this great collection can be conveniently studied and enjoyed.

CHAPTER ONE

The New Art

Photography is, like the Victoria and Albert Museum, often thought of as a Victorian invention. However, both the medium and the institution were formed somewhat earlier – and so was the individual who brought them together. The story starts in 1835.

Henry Cole (1808–82), who founded what is now the V&A, grew up in the Age of Reform. He made friendships in his youth with such glittering talents as the Radical MP Charles Buller (1806–48), the philosopher John Stuart Mill (1806–73) and the novelist Thomas Love Peacock (1785–1866). At the end of his long life, Cole – by then Sir Henry Cole KCB – reflected:

> In 1882 half a century will have passed since the first great Reform Bill became law, in obedience to a popular demand so stern as to be irresistible, that the worn-out fictitious representation of places like Old Sarum and Gatton, which had lost their populations, should be abolished, and that the thousands in Manchester, Birmingham, and other places in the North should be duly represented in Parliament. The Reform Bill led to many other reforms: Abolition of Religious Tests, Municipal Corporation Reform, Abolition of Slavery, Reform of the Poor Laws; and, I venture to say, that the Reform of the Public Record System, exposed by Charles Buller, could not have received proper public attention before the year 1835; when any powers of action I possessed for public work were first called out.[1]

Cole's biographer, Elizabeth Bonython, has explained what happened in 1835. He had joined the Record Commission as a young man, but friction between Cole and the corrupt administration during 1835 led to his dismissal on 5 December that year. No longer a civil servant, Cole was able to campaign against the enormities of the system. A select committee of the House of Commons was appointed in 1836. As a result of its report, Cole was reinstated to his position two years later. He remained there until 1852, when he moved into the world of art education and museums. However, 'the affair of the Record Commission made Cole famous, some might have said infamous. He learnt the uses of journalism and publicity, and people in high places began to hear of him'.[2]

The Age of Reform touched everything, including art education. On 14 July 1835 a select committee was appointed 'to inquire into the best means of extending a knowledge of the Arts and of the Principles of Design among the People (especially

1. William Henry Fox Talbot (British, 1800–77). **Lace**, 1844. Photogenic drawing (negative). Plate XX in *The Pencil of Nature*, 1844–6. 6 5/16 × 8 7/16 in (16 × 21.4 cm). Bought 1939. RC.R.1. National Art Library.

the Manufacturing Population) of the Country'. The committee chairman was William Ewart (1798–1869), Radical MP for Liverpool. Ewart was a back-bencher of extraordinary achievements. There was much to reform. Among many other interventions, Ewart carried a bill in 1837 that abolished capital punishment for horse, cattle and sheep stealing. He campaigned successfully for free libraries, public museums and galleries for the enjoyment of the mass of the population. Ewart and those who supported him were trying, Janet Minihan has written, 'to effect a complete reorientation of British art. They wanted what had been for centuries the pastime of the rich to become a familiar aspect of the daily lives of the people'.[3]

Ewart's committee was keen to outdo the French and to learn from the Germans. The first – and crucial – witness was Dr G.F. Waagen, distinguished Director of Berlin's Royal Museum, who came before the committee three times in July and August 1835. He spoke of Prussia's applied art institute in Berlin. It had a library, a collection of working models 'representing the newest discoveries in Europe, and particularly in England', and plaster casts of ornamental decoration and sculpture. He spoke of improving industrial competitiveness through good design, in a way that also sounded like the blueprint of a good society: 'In former times the artists were more workmen, and the workmen were more artists, as in the time of Raphael, and it is very desirable to restore this happy connexion'. 'How would you restore it?', he was asked. By creating great collections, he answered. These should represent both ancient and modern art. They should show the development of each art from master to pupil and generation to generation: 'such an arrangement, by following the spirit of the times and the genius of the artists, would provide a harmonious influence upon the mind of the spectator'.[4]

Dr Waagen urged the need for special exhibitions, regular purchasing from contemporary artists and 'a national museum of British art'. He said that artists should work on public building projects, such as the new Houses of Parliament.[5] The select committee recommended the foundation of an institute of the kind that Waagen had described. It also stated 'that the opening of public galleries for the people should, as much as possible, be encouraged'.[6] In the next decades Britain was to emulate its continental neighbours – most particularly its main commercial rival, France – by opening public museums and galleries up and down the land.

Elsewhere in England, another member of the Reform Parliament of 1832–4, William Henry Fox Talbot FRS (1800–77), had dropped politics in favour of a pursuit for which he was far more gifted – experimental science. Talbot's inspiring story has been told many times: the brilliant natural scientist and polymath who took his wife on honeymoon to the shores of Lake Como in 1833; who relaxed there by sketching the scenery with the aid of a camera lucida, but discovered his own lack of facility for even the simplest kind of drawing. The camera lucida was an aid which allowed the artist to view both scene and drawing paper simultaneously. Talbot vowed to find a

2. Calvert Richard Jones (1804–77). **Lime Leaf**, *c.*1845 Photogenic drawing. 8⅛ × 6⅜ in (20.8 × 16.5 cm). Bought 1983. Ph.66–1983.

way for nature not only to draw her own image, but also to leave a permanent imprint on the paper. At Lacock Abbey in Wiltshire he used his knowledge of chemistry – especially the light-sensitive properties of silver salts – to carry out a series of astonishing experiments. Talbot told the story in *The Pencil of Nature*, published in instalments in 1844–6. He refers here to the camera obscura, a more sophisticated drawing device. A lens and reflecting mirror cast the image of a view downwards on to a sheet of paper, where the outlines could be traced. The 'camera' was invented long before photography. Talbot recalled how

3. Attributed to M. DE STE CROIX (French, active 1839). **Parliament Street from Trafalgar Square**, 1839. Daguerreotype. 5¼ × 6¾ in (13.3 × 17.2 cm). Bought 1986. Ph.1–1986.

> during the brilliant summer of 1835 in England I made new attempts to obtain pictures of buildings with the Camera Obscura; and having devised a process which gave additional sensibility to the paper, viz. by giving it repeated alternate washes of salt and silver, and using it in a moist state, I succeeded in reducing the time necessary for obtaining an image with the Camera Obscura on a bright day to ten minutes. But these pictures, though very pretty, were very small, being quite miniatures.[7]

Talbot also made direct impressions of lace, like the famous image from *The Pencil of Nature* shown here (Plate 1). Plants and leaves drew themselves on light-sensitive paper in the sunshine, in startling, intricate clarity. Talbot grasped that these impressions could be used as what he termed negatives. His novel paper impressions could be printed from, to make 'positives'. A wonderful example is the lime leaf, its organic structure even finer than lace, by his friend Calvert Richard Jones (Plate 2).

The summer of 1835 was brilliant in every sense, for Talbot created the essentials of photography as it was to be practised for the next 150 years. He carried out the decisive experiments and, with his friends and colleagues, thought up many of the words. He wrote in *The Pencil of Nature* of 'the New Art, which has been since named Photography'.[8]

It seems astounding that Talbot should have invented photography in 1835 and then put his revolutionary experiments aside, but he did, moving restlessly on to new topics. However, his attention was drastically refocused in 1839 by news from Paris. An extraordinary invention by Louis-Jacques-Mandé Daguerre (1787–1851) was reported in the *Gazette de France* for 6 January 1839. The leading scientist François Arago announced Daguerre's discovery to the Académie des Sciences the next day. Talbot responded by arranging for Britain's leading scientist, Michael Faraday, to announce *his* photographic invention to the Royal Institution in London on 25 January. The battle of the inventions would be fought out over the next decade and a half, with Talbot ultimately victorious. However, in the beginning, Daguerre and the French made the running. With characteristic *éclat*, the secrets of the Daguerreotype were disclosed in Paris by the French government on 14 August 1839. The new invention would be free to the world, with a small exception – Daguerre had taken

out a patent in England and Wales the previous day.

The English did not have to wait long for the arrival of specimens of Daguerre's process, nor for a man who would demonstrate the technique before their very eyes. A M. de Ste Croix is reported to have conducted demonstrations, first in London and afterwards in Birmingham and Liverpool – but then disappears mysteriously from history.[9] The Frenchman gave his first display on 13 September, the Catholic feastday of the Holy Cross ('Fête de Ste Croix'), and it has been suggested that he adopted a pseudonym, perhaps anticipating the litigation over patent rights which duly occurred.[10] A Welsh newspaper, *The Cambrian* (20 September 1839), was among many which covered the story:

> The Daguerreotype – The first experiments made in this country with the instrument and process of M. Daguerre, were exhibited on Friday by M. Ste Croix who has just arrived from Paris, in the presence of a select number of scientific men and artists. The apparatus is similar to that employed in the camera obscura. The invention is a great improvement on photogenic drawing, inasmuch as the representations of existing objects are more perfect, the minute details are accurately preserved, and to a slight degree the tints of colours secured. The shadow is not taken on paper, but on a thin plate of copper, plated with silver...[11]

The correspondent describes the complex procedures of sensitizing the polished silver plate, including treatments with vapour of iodine before and after the exposure of 20 minutes, and the result:

> the plate exhibits a perfect representation of the object or objects which have been conveyed into the focus of the camera obscura box... the picture produced was a beautiful miniature representation of houses, pathway, sky, &c., resembling a beautiful mezzotint.[12]

Parliament Street from Trafalgar Square (Plate 3) was first attributed to De Ste Croix by Dr David Thomas, and first shown in modern times at the V&A in the exhibition *'From Today Painting is Dead': The Origins of Photography*, in 1972. It is among the handful of images that introduced Britons to photography and to the photographic representation of their metropolis. As is characteristic of the Daguerreotype, the scene is reversed, with the Royal Banqueting House appearing on the right-hand side of the street. Some of the houses and the statue of Charles I still stand on the same spot. So do the iron bollards, cast with the cipher of William IV, in the foreground. Under magnification the Daguerreotype reveals more. The first-floor windows of a chophouse had been thrown open on the bright autumn day. The globes of the street-lamps contained advertisements for tea. However, the illusion of reality perfectly captured is just that – an illusion. The exposure was perhaps long enough for a whole crowd to

4. ANTOINE-FRANÇOISE-JEAN CLAUDET (worked London, born France, 1797–1867). **Andrew Pritchard**, 18 July 1843. Daguerreotype. Measurements: image size, 2¾ × 2¼ in (6.6 × 5.7 cm); closed case size, 3¾ × 3¼ in (9.5 × 8.2 cm). Given by Miss E.M. Spiller, 1939. Ph.57–1939.

have strolled through the scene without leaving a trace on the plate. The few visible humans – the first Britons to be recorded in a surviving photograph – are hansom-cab drivers (who may have been paid to stay put), and a figure slumped among the bollards (who may have been drunk).

Daguerre's process became practicable for portraiture, and therefore commercially viable, thanks to the contributions of other inventors and scientists. A French-born Londoner, Antoine-Françoise-Jean Claudet FRS (1797–1867), took up photography in 1840 as, according to a contemporary, a 'philosophic pursuit… and henceforth, literally, his days were devoted to the practice, his nights to the theory of the new art and science'.[13] Like Talbot, he possessed a broad range of scientific skills. 'When at first chemistry had to be called in aid, he was a chemist… When, later, optics had to be appealed to, he was a mathematician; when chemical science was to be invoked – he was an ingenious mechanician; when art was required, he was an artist of consummate taste'.[14] His experiments included taking 'an impression of black lace by the light of the full moon in two minutes, and by the light of the stars in fifteen minutes; an impression of a sculpted figure by the light of a candle in fifteen minutes, and the same by the light of a lamp in five minutes; and an image of the moon in four seconds'.[15] In the early days of the medium, there was a race to cut exposure times and another to capture newly possible subjects. Claudet found a method of accelerating the Daguerreotype process by using bromine and chloride of iodine. This enabled him to take vivid portraits, like that of Andrew Pritchard (Plate 4), in just a few seconds. Pritchard (1804–82) was himself an inventor and entrepreneur, proprietor of an emporium for scientific instruments in London's Ludgate Circus. He was famous for making jewel lenses and Claudet used them, so they probably knew each other as business associates.

Although generally a studio medium, Daguerreotypists also produced images out of doors and overseas. Plate 5 may well be the first Daguerreotype of fly-fishing. It is also an authentic ancestor of the family snapshot of later times. It was taken by Horatio Ross, a sensationally gifted British sportsman (best known as a steeplechaser and shot), who took up the medium as an amateur in 1845. The photographer's son 'Hoddy' (the nickname of Horatio Ross, Jr), is shown fishing with a ghilly on a Scottish salmon river. The landscape is slightly brown in tint and the sky is blue. The blue was not painted, but a happy optical accident. When a subject has a high level of contrast, the brighter tone can reverse, in this case into a natural blue. This effect, called solarization, was deliberately used by the Surrealists, as we shall see.

Talbot had also drastically improved his process. In 1841 he discovered the 'latent image', an invisible impression in the negative that could be 'developed' – made fully visible – chemically. He patented this vital improvement as the 'calotype' (or 'beautiful print', from the Greek *kalos*). His breakthrough greatly cut exposure times. Now the calotype could challenge the Daguerreotype both in portraiture and

5. HORATIO ROSS (British, 1801–86). **Hoddy and John Munro Fishing at Flaipool**, 1847. Daguerreotype. 4½ × 5¾ in (10.7 × 14.5 cm). Given by Major Ross. 244–1946.

BROWN
J. PLAYER
25
CONGREVE MATCH
FANCY
& BLACKING

6. CALVERT RICHARD JONES (British, 1804–77). **Study of a Bridge, Bristol**, *c.*1845. Calotype. 6⅞ × 8⅞ in (17.5 × 22.3 cm). Bought 1983. Ph.46–1983.

the crisp reality of the street, as rendered here by Talbot's friend Calvert Richard Jones (Plate 6). Perhaps Jones remembered, when composing his richly filled urban scene, Talbot's words:

> In examining photographic pictures of a certain degree of perfection, the use of a large lens is recommended, such as elderly persons frequently employ in reading. This magnifies the objects two or three times, and often discloses a multitude of minute details, which were previously unobserved and unsuspected. It frequently happens, moreover – and this is one of the charms of photography – that the operator himself discovers on examination, perhaps long afterwards, that he has depicted many things he had no notion of at the time. Sometimes inscriptions and dates are found upon the buildings, or printed placards, most irrelevant, are discovered on their walls.[16]

Calotype portraiture and figure studies flourished in the Edinburgh studio of Hill and Adamson, which was surely the finest in Europe in the 1840s. The unprecedented, hybrid nature of 'the New Art' was perfectly expressed by the combination of the established painter David Octavius Hill and the brilliant young chemist Robert Adamson. In contrast to the cold precision of the Daguerreotype portrait, their calotypes offered a russet complexion and the lively character of a sketch (Plate 7). The pleasing warm tone is the optical/chemical effect of printing out the positive by sunlight. The negative and a sheet of positive paper, in close contact, were placed in the sunshine in a printing frame (Figure 1). The sketchy impression is the hallmark of the paper negative, which was relatively coarse compared to such later negative materials as glass and film. Hill and Adamson exhibited a group of their works at the Royal Scottish Academy in 1845 as 'calotype portrait sketches'.

(right) Figure 1. JOHN DILLWYN LLEWELYN (British, 1810–82). **Mrs D.L**, 1853. Salted paper print from glass negative. 5 × 4 in (12.7 × 10.2 cm). From Bessie Llewelyn's album, X.1. Bought 1984. Ph.129–1984.

Another of photography's characteristic colours arrived in the 1840s – the Prussian blue of the 'Cyanotype' or blueprint. The Cyanotype process was invented by Talbot's associate Sir John Herschel FRS in 1842. The first woman photographer, Anna Atkins – already a skilled technical illustrator – produced the first photographically illustrated book. Her three-volume *British Algae: Cyanotype Impressions* was privately issued in instalments, beginning in October 1843. Botanical specimens and, as here, text were laid on paper impregnated with iron salts and exposed to sunlight for a few minutes (Plate 8). This produced a faint image that was brought

7. David Octavius Hill (British, 1802–70) and Robert Adamson (British, 1821–48). **Master Grierson**, *c.*1845. Calotype. 7⅞ × 5¾ in (20.2 × 14.8 cm). Given by Sir Theodore Martin, 1868. In album X.55 (ii). 67.379.

out to a rich blue and made permanent simply by washing the paper in plain water. The process became the standard means of reproducing the drawings of architects and engineers. Nowadays it is often used in classrooms as a satisfying way to teach children the elements of photography.

Colour entered photography by another route. Licences to practise the Daguerreotype process became available in London only in 1846. Now some Daguerreotype studios teamed up with the miniature painters, who had observed the growth of the new photographic processes with concern for their own livelihoods. The painted Daguerreotype was a speciality of William Edward Kilburn (Plate 9), who was among a number of photographers licensed to open Daguerreotype studios in 1846. His advertisements were printed in *The Athenaeum*, among those for singing lessons, phantasmagoria lantern slides, offers of fine engravings, cures for stammering and Roman coins: 'The likeness taken by the photographic process serves merely as a sketch for the miniature, which is painted by M. Mansion, whose productions on Ivory are so celebrated in Paris. They have when finished all the delicacy of an elaborate miniature, with the infallible accuracy of expression only obtainable by the photographic process''.[17] Three hand-coloured Daguerreotypes by Kilburn were exhibited at the Great Exhibition of 1851.[18]

In the 1840s photography began its ascent to commercial success and social centrality. It remained relatively expensive, however. A Daguerreotype portrait by M. Claudet, who imported his plates from France, cost £1.3s.6d. This was a little more than the average urban weekly wage.[19] Moreover, the medium – however magical – had arrived in hard times. The inventions of Daguerre and Talbot were protected in England by patents and practised only under licence. Even so, Talbot lost money, Hill and Adamson are unlikely to have made any, and Calvert Richard Jones wrote to Talbot in 1846: 'if I cannot make some arrangement with you concerning Photography, I shall be obliged to turn my thoughts to something else', adding 'My Poverty and not my will consents.'[20] Talbot's wonderful *The Pencil of Nature* was not a commercial success either. He tried to promote his invention in *The Art Union* in June 1846, but Talbot's prints – pasted on to the magazine's pages – faded disappointingly. Potential customers continued to regard his invention sceptically. The library of the Government School of Design subscribed to *The Art Union* and, as that library formed the beginning of today's National Art Library at the V&A,[21] the Museum's Photography Collection could be said to have begun in 1846, unpromisingly, with a faded calotype. Talbot's process remained a private avocation, rather than a trusted technology. Significantly, although C.H. Wilson of the School of Design collected Talbotypes himself, the school's library did not subscribe to *The Pencil of Nature*.[22] The Museum did not acquire Talbot's masterwork until 1939, as we shall see in chapter five. The progress of photography did not, of course, take place in an economic vacuum.

British
Ferns.

8. ANNA ATKINS (British, 1797–1871). Title Page: **British Ferns**, c.1854. Cyanotype. 13⅝ × 9⅞ in (22.8 × 18.4 cm). Bought 1982. Ph.379–1981.

Photography began to prosper only in the upturn ushered in by the Great Exhibition of 1851. The Great Exhibition of Works of Industry of All Nations included a very significant showing of photography. A distinguished international jury described it as 'the most remarkable discovery of modern times – the art of photography – and never before was there so rich a collection of photographic pictures brought together, the products of England, France, Austria and America'.[23] Among those honoured by the Exhibition's Commissioners were Claudet, David Octavius Hill and Kilburn. Hill showed in Section XXX, the Fine Arts Section, the others in Section X, 'Philosophical Instruments and Objects Depending on their Use': that is to say, with astronomy, optics, light, heat, electricity and so on. Classifying 'the New Art' was problematic from the first moment that anyone seriously tried. However, in 1851 photography achieved critical mass. It emerged from the Great Exhibition as something more than a commercial portraiture machine or a gizmo of the scientifically gifted.

Henry Cole, by this time Chairman of the Fine Arts Committee of the Society of Arts, was a prime mover in planning the Great Exhibition. It was he who proposed to Prince Albert that it should be international, that is truly 'Great'. Indeed, the Great Exhibition was unprecedented in size, scope and profits. Out of its success came new opportunities for Cole himself, and out of the profits came the means to realize them. First, however, he took a leading role in organizing the photographic documentation of the displays. This was the most ambitious use of photography so far attempted anywhere: over 20,000 prints were produced from 155 negatives by five photographers.[24] They illustrated 140 four-volume presentation sets of the *Reports by the Juries of the Great Exhibition*. These grand volumes, in crimson morocco bindings and blue watered-silk doublures, were published by the Royal Commissioners of the Great Exhibition.

Cole took a decisive role in ensuring that the photographs were not only well taken, but also, a critically important issue, well printed. He will have known that fading prints had undermined Talbot's efforts to popularize his invention in the 1840s. There was a very serious falling-out between the Executive Committee and Talbot, and Cole must have played a key part in this bruising encounter. The important contract for supplying the photographs was withdrawn from Nicholas Henneman, whom Talbot had set up in business. Instead the photographs would be printed in France under the supervision of a Paris-based Englishman, Robert Bingham. Talbot's paper negative process was abandoned for much of the work too. Several photographers preferred to use negatives of glass coated with albumen. (Two of these albumen-on-glass negatives of the Great Exhibition are now in the Photography Collection.) The clarity and tonal richness of Plates 10 and 11 show how very well some, if not entirely all, of the 20,000 prints have survived. Plate 11 illustrates equestrian royalty – Marochetti's sculpture of Richard I disappearing into the mists –

Figure 2. Attributed to CHARLES THURSTON THOMPSON (1816–68). **Henry Cole and Richard Redgrave, Gore House Garden**, 1854. Albumen print. 6⅜ × 8 in (16.2 × 20.3 cm). From Marian Cole's album. Given by the Friends of the V&A, 1987. Ph.835–1987.

(oppposite)
9. WILLIAM EDWARD KILBURN (British, active 1846–62). **Portrait of a Lady**, 1851. Hand-tinted and gilt Daguerreotype in plush-lined papier-mâché case, embossed with the studio's name and the Royal arms. 4⅞ × 4 in (12.5 × 10 cm). Given by J.L. Nevinson, 1939. 3–1939.

and steam power. This confrontation between art and industry in Hyde Park suggests that for photography to be (mostly) classified with science, rather than fine art, was a declaration of its significance and vigour.

Talbot exhibited nothing at the Great Exhibition. It should have been the occasion at which his genius was finally vindicated and honoured, but his invention was now developing in the hands of others.

The report of the jury on photography was even-handed and discerning, praising American Daguerreotypes and French calotypes above their English counterparts. It was clairvoyant in imagining the future perfection of colour photography and it made this accurate prediction: 'It is likely that time will show that this beautiful compound of art and science will essentially cast its weight into the balance of art, and in future render itself more and more inseparable from and essential to her interests'.[25] Soon afterwards photography began to establish itself as the major means of documenting art and architecture. However, the jurors looked further ahead and saw a time when photography would be able to capture the 'scenes daily passing around us' and that would introduce 'a new era in pictorial representation'[26] – as we shall see in chapters four and five.

10. Attributed to Claude-Marie Ferrier (French, 1811–89). **Reports by the Juries of the Great Exhibition**, 1851. Volume II (Westmacott set), 1852, opp. p.763, 'View of Transept, Looking South'. National Art Library Special Collections, AR B–C, vol.II.

(right)
11. Attributed to Claude-Marie Ferrier (French, 1811–89). **Reports by the Juries of the Great Exhibition**, 1851. Volume II (Department of Practical Art set), 1852, opp. p.495, 'Agricultural Implements, Garrett & Sons'. National Art Library Special Collections, AR B–C, vol.II.

Out of the Great Exhibition of 1851 came profits of £186,000 and, both metaphorically and literally, a new cultural landscape. Guided by Prince Albert, and with Government help, the Exhibition Commissioners bought 86 acres of land, including some houses and market gardens, in the area south of Hyde Park. Here Prince Albert envisaged a new cultural quarter. Just before the Great Exhibition closed, the Government spent five thousand pounds on buying contemporary applied art exhibits from the show. These were to be added to the casts and so on already acquired by the Government School of Design in Somerset House. This first school had been followed by some 20 more, established in manufacturing centres around the country. However, they were embroiled in constant disputes for most of the 1840s. In 1852 Henry Cole took control of the Schools of Design, and their incipient museum. He was appointed General Superintendent of the Board of Trade's new Department of Practical Art. The painter Richard Redgrave became Art Superintendent. Cole and Redgrave were photographed together in the grounds of Gore House, just south of Hyde Park, in 1854 (Figure 2). Cole set to work in 1852 at speed, and photography was part of the enterprise from the beginning.

The medium had developed rapidly following the 1851 Exhibition. Already in 1851 the sculptor/inventor Frederick Scott Archer introduced a process that combined many of the best features of the Daguerreotype and calotype. Archer's collodion on glass negative combined the coveted clarity of the French process with the ready repeatability of the English one. If the negative was exposed in the camera

12. Ludwig Belitski (German, 1830–1902). **15th and 16th Century Venetian Vases and Glasses**, *c.*1855. Liegnitz, Minutolisches Institut. Salted paper print, published 1855 9 × 7¼ in (22.8 × 18.4 cm). Given by H.R.H. The Prince Consort, 1855. 36.077.

while the sensitive coating was still wet, the new process was also dramatically superior to its predecessors in speed. The wet collodion process was usually used with relatively glossy printing paper coated with albumen (based on the transparency and adhesiveness of egg white). The new negative rapidly drove the older processes from the field.

Many photographs made with the new technique were shown at the first exhibition in the world devoted solely to photography: *Recent Specimens of Photography*, at the Society of Arts in December 1852. The exhibition included many photographs taken at the Crystal Palace for the Royal Commissioners. (Works by the different photographers involved in that project can be identified from the details given in the catalogue of the Society of Arts' exhibition.) Henry Cole may have persuaded the Commissioners to lend the Great Exhibition photographs, to show how these things should be done, and he is personally listed as owner of a view of the Louvre by F. Martens. Among the 779 exhibits were views of Egypt, the first photographic prints of Egypt, taken by Flaubert's friend Maxime du Camp.

The first seventeen instalments of Du Camp's *Egypte, Nubie, Palestine et Syrie* (Paris, 1852) were bought (for £18) for the Museum on 19 April 1853. The transaction was recorded in another innovation of the Cole regime, a Diary of Books, Prints, &c., Inspected, Purchased for, or Presented to the Art Library, begun on 28 January 1853.[27] Du Camp's other instalments were bought as they came out. The Photography Collection began in earnest in 1853. It was part of the Art Library, later the National Art Library, which Richard Redgrave spoke of in a lecture in the same year as one of the four instruments of the Department of Practical Art, the others being the schools of design, public lectures and the museum.[28] To begin with, the Art Library acquired photographs strictly of works of art. Blanquard-Evrard's *Mélanges Photographiques* ('Photographic Mixtures') arrived for consideration on 9 July 1853. Only two of the 21 photographs were bought (at 2s.6d. each). They were Charles Marville's photographs of the classical sculpture galleries at the Louvre.

Royal patronage continued, with the presentation to the Museum by Prince Albert of some of the most eloquent photographic interpretations of art objects ever made (Plate 12). In 1855 he gave 150 photographs from a German collection of applied arts that had anticipated Cole's new enterprise. Produced and published by the Minutolisches Institut in Liegnitz, Silesia, these brilliantly lit photographs were intended to provide craftsmen with clear illustrations of the best technical models. This again was the first instalment in a series.

With publications like this, and such treasures as Du Camp's album, Cole began to assemble perhaps the greatest of all 'museums without walls'. This major aspect of the Museum's collection has been thoroughly appraised by Dr Anthony Hamber in *'A Higher Branch of the Art': Photography of the Fine Arts in England, 1839–1880* (1996).

In 1853 Cole began to use photography to record exhibitions and the works of art temporarily lent to his new museum. An *Exhibition of Decorative Furniture* at Gore House was recorded by a lithographer-turned-photographer, Francis Bedford (1816–94), and by Charles Thurston Thompson (1816–68), an engraver-turned-photographer. Thurston Thompson, an old associate of Cole's, had worked with Bingham on the production of the photographic prints for the *Reports by the Juries* and afterwards studied with him in Paris. Thurston Thompson himself appears, reflected with his camera and a basket of utensils, in a Venetian mirror that he photographed in the grounds of Gore House (Plate 13). He appears to be looking studiously at his watch to determine when to replace the lens cap of the camera and thus conclude the exposure. The exposure had to be long to capture the rich detail of the mirror frame. Is this an intentional self-portrait? If so, it matches what is known of Thurston Thompson. His industrious career is said to have yielded 10,000 negatives of works of art.[29] He also made photographs of Brompton before it was transformed and studies of trees in Surrey. He supervised the British photographic contributions to the international exhibitions of 1855 and 1867. He was 'a man of extensive and varied culture, possessing a most discriminating taste and judgement; but, withal, modest and unassuming. As a private friend he was a rarely amiable man, possessing an unusually winning and conciliatory deportment'.[30] He was the first in the long line of dedicated Museum photographers in South Kensington that continues today.

Photographs and photographers were present from the very beginning of the Museum's history. Less than 20 years after 'the brilliant summer of 1835', a new medium, a new museum, and its forceful founding director, had converged on a new site in Brompton, West London. Henry Cole renamed the district South Kensington, which he felt had more social tone.

13. CHARLES THURSTON THOMPSON (British, 1816–68). **Venetian Mirror c.1700 from the Collection of John Webb**, 1853. Albumen print. 9 × 6⅜ in (22.8 × 16.3 cm). Official Museum photograph. 39.833.

34

CHAPTER TWO

'A Vibrant Populist Enterprise'

In 1856 Cole's young museum was given land and buildings on the present site. It opened its doors for the first time as the South Kensington Museum in 1857. The American scholar of museum history Michael Conforti has recently written:

> In South Kensington's earliest years there was an enthusiastic trial-and-error atmosphere to the place. The confident, pragmatic approach to operations by Cole and his staff was to become an Anglo-American museum tradition. Both enjoy common origins in the liberal, civic-minded social philosophy of the time, and both were supported by a rising business class.[1]

Cole aimed to achieve many of the goals that Dr Waagen had set out in the summer of 1835: systematically acquired and displayed collections, broad public access, special exhibitions, new buildings decorated by artists and even a National Gallery of British Art. South Kensington was meant to be a museum for the masses, with free days, evening opening hours and an educational mission:

> Everything shall be... made as intelligible as possible by descriptive labels. Other collections may attract the learned to explore them, but these will be arranged so clearly that they may woo the ignorant to examine them. This Museum will be like a book with its pages always open, not shut.[2]

While the collections were still forming, at dramatic speed, Cole published catalogues to make them better known and understood. Special exhibitions attracted large numbers. The Museum was open free from 10 am to 10 pm on Mondays, Tuesdays and Saturdays. (These hours embraced the Art Library, for which there was an admission fee of sixpence.) Wednesdays, Thursdays and Fridays (10 am to 5 pm) were 'students days', for the School of Design (later to become the Royal College of Art) had also moved to South Kensington; general visitors had to pay a small admission charge. Sunday opening was still a long way in the future for all museums.

Just as the School of Design's collection had been circulated (from 1844), so too were the Museum's collections toured to regional centres. This was carried out initially in a converted railway train, which travelled to manufacturing cities and stayed for several months. The first major Circulating Exhibition contained some 430 specimens plus 150 framed drawings, photographs and prints. It travelled to Birmingham in February 1855. Cole lobbied to improve public transport to South Kensington. The new buildings were opened by Queen Victoria, accompanied by

14. John Watson (British, active 1850s). **Academic Study**, 1855. Albumen print from collodion negative. 13¼ × 10¼ in (33.9 × 26 cm). Bought 1856. 36.373.

Prince Albert, on 22 June 1857 and boasted, among other attractions, the first ever museum restaurant. The South Kensington Museum was really a complex of institutions: the Museum of Education, the Museum of Animal Products, the Museum of Ornamental Art, the National Art Training School, the Patent Museum, and the offices of the Department of Science and Art. The Architectural Museum was added in 1863. 'South Kensington', Conforti sums up, 'was a vibrant populist enterprise...'[3]

15. William Lake Price (British, c.1810–96). **The First of September**, 1855. Albumen print from collodion negative. 11⅞ × 9⅞ in (30 × 25.2 cm). Bought 1856. 36.375.

As well as masterminding the new museum, Cole was responsible for organizing the British contribution to the Paris Exposition Universelle of 1855. Following, but vastly extending, the photographic record of the Great Exhibition, Charles Thurston Thompson and Robert J. Bingham used large wet collodion-on-glass negatives to make superb photographs of the exhibition and its buildings. Their survey included the famous pavilion that Gustave Courbet had erected, in defiance of the authorities, to exhibit his paintings. For French photography, 1855 was the equivalent of 1851 for the British. It included the first substantial showing of international photography in France. It was part of Class XXVI, 'Drawing and Modelling Applied to Industry, Letter-Press and Copper-Plate Printing, Photography'. The display in the Palais de l'Industrie set a new standard of elegance in its arrangements and in the sophistication of its exhibits. Almost half a century later Nadar would recall with rapture the expressions of the mime artist Debureau fils, photographed by Adrien Tournachon, and the masterpieces of other French pioneers.[4] The display changed the climate of opinion about the medium.

Henry Cole must have seen the exhibition, although his diaries for 1855 are missing. (His family may have suppressed them because they did not show Cole in a favourable light.) Certainly, something or perhaps several things happened that made Henry Cole focus on photography even more than before. In 1856 he appointed Charles Thurston Thompson as Superintendent of Photography and, as John Physick has remarked, 'the first museum photographic service came into being'.[5] This began a powerful programme of recording works of art, architecture and design in the interests of public education, becoming the lead programme in the field. Secondly, Cole took up photography himself. He photographed his family, friends and servants, his newly acquired weekend cottage in Surrey, and the places he visited on holiday or business. He was a typical amateur, hopefully or recklessly trying subjects that most professionals did not – such as the dark interiors of his cottage. Marian Cole's album, which contains many photographs by her husband, was given to the Photography Collection by the Friends of the V&A in 1987.[6] Thirdly, Cole began the Museum's collection of photography as an independent art medium.

On 22 January 1856 Cole and Thurston Thompson visited an *Exhibition of Photographs and Daguerreotypes* at the Gallery of the Society of Water Colour Painters, 5 Pall Mall East.[7] It was the third annual exhibition of the Photographic Society of London and contained a good showing of prints by Thurston Thompson himself. Cole

Figure 3. William Henry Lake Price (British, *c.*1810–96). **Don Quixote in his Study**, 1855. Albumen print from glass negative. 12¾ × 11⅛ in (32.4 × 28.3 cm). Bought 1976 3–1976

(opposite) 16. Robert Howlett (British, 1831–58). **Valley of the Mole**, 1855. Albumen print from collodion negative. 7⅜ × 9¼ in (19 × 23.7 cm). Bought 1856. 36.353

was not exclusively interested in the photography of art. He bought the first art photographs for the Museum's collection. These include the *Academic Study* by John Watson, who ran J. Watson & Co., professional photographers in Regent Street (Plate 14). The relatively high price of £1.1s. for this photograph presumably reflects the professional model's fee. The speed of the wet collodion process allowed models to pose with a new naturalness. The title *Academic Study* was perhaps intended to emphasize the lofty purpose of this photograph, as an aid to artists, in contrast to the lubricious photographic 'studies' which had already become a major branch of commercial photography.[8] Watson photographed the model in *profil perdu*. The focus delicately describes the back and hips. The shawl, mirror, dresser and bowl of roses receive less definition.

The other 21 photographs that Cole bought ranged in price from 4s. to 10s.6d. Cole noted in his diary 'a number of good still life' and bought V.A. Prout's *Christmas Fare* and William Lake Price's *The First of September* (Plate 15). Lake Price, trained as a painter and lithographer, carefully toned his photograph, ensuring that the print has remained in perfect preservation to this day. Its autumnal colour evokes the first day of the grouse-shooting season. Cole added in his diary: 'the dramatic Scenes I think failures'. An example of the latter is Lake Price's composition *Don Quixote in his Study* (Figure 3), which emulates the antiquarian costume studies exhibited by painters at the time.

Cole preferred to buy Robert Howlett's *Valley of the Mole* (Plate 16) and Francis Bedford's *The Baptistery, Canterbury Cathedral* (Plate 17). These works possessed a more subtle artistry. Photographers had adopted the themes of Britain's major tradition of watercolour painting and given them a new twist. Bedford's Canterbury photograph includes the staffage of an old man and a boy, a wiry thorn bush, blowing blossoms, and summer flowers among the grass. The hallowed Picturesque subject, a mainstay of the watercolour medium's topographical tradition, is accompanied by a host of intricate circumstantial details and the breeze of actuality.

How did the 1850s see these photographs? The photographer and critic Thomas Sutton wrote in 1854 that 'the true poetry of photography lies not in portraiture... but in views; by which I mean, of course, not garden gates, stiff houses and spick and span modern buildings, but such grand scenes or artistic sites as a painter would select, with the wide world before him to choose from'.[9] Another critic wrote of Bedford's *The Baptistery, Canterbury Cathedral*: 'the appearance of the foliage combined with the architecture is exquisitely beautiful. If he uses, as I suppose, the common collodion process [he did], what an illustration of the truth that manipulation is less than taste in photography; and that a man must be an artist to get good results'.[10] The meaning of the word 'artist' was shifting in this period. Here it has apparently been used to signify gifts of sensibility rather than craft accomplishments.

French photographers also pursued fugitive natural effects, with dramatic results. They took on the same subjects as their contemporaries of the Barbizon School. Both André Giroux and Gustave Le Gray had trained as painters and both won medals for their photography at the Exposition Universelle. They enlivened their landscapes and seascapes with richly clouded skies. However, Giroux preferred to work with the paper negative process (Plate 18). Like the 'Pictorialist' photographers half a century later, he treated the negative as merely a starting point. He worked on its surface with pen and ink, creating highlights in the meadows and the foliage of the trees, and filling the pools of marshy water with textures. He also added the clouds. These were

17. Francis Bedford (British, 1816–94). **The Baptistery, Canterbury Cathedral**, 1855. Albumen print from wet collodion negative. 9⅛ × 7⅛ in (23.3 × 18.1 cm). Bought 1856. 36.363.

'printed-in' from a second negative. Gustave Le Gray used wet collodion on glass negatives (Plate 19). He became celebrated as the first photographer to capture the speed of moving waves and scudding clouds, but he also used separate negatives for the two parts of his compositions. Negatives were too sensitive to the blue parts of the spectrum and it was normally impossible to record both ground and sky simultaneously on the same plate. Photographers employed various stratagems to compensate for the technical limitations of the medium – as, of course, they continue to do today.

18. André Giroux (French, 1801–79). **The Ponds at Obtevoz (Rhône)**, *c.*1855. Salted paper print. 10⅝ × 13¼ in (27 × 33.5 cm). C.H. Townshend Bequest, 1868. 68.011.

The South Kensington Museum, having begun its collection of the art of photography in 1856, went on to hold its first international exhibition of photography two years later. The Museum simultaneously presented the annual exhibitions of the Photographic Society of London and its Parisian counterpart, La Société française de photographie. The exhibitions of the Photographic Society of London (patrons HM The Queen and HRH The Prince Consort) included the works of distinguished amateurs – artists and scientists, lawyers and manufacturers. Contributors included both the committed photographers of the first wave in the 1840s, such as J.D. Llewelyn and Horatio Ross, and of the second wave of the 1850s, such talents as Francis Bedford, C.L. Dodgson ('Lewis Carroll'), Roger Fenton, Robert Howlett, Lake Price, Oscar Gustav Rejlander, Henry Taylor and Benjamin Brecknell Turner.

Cole laconically recorded in his diary on 12 February 1858: 'Museum: Queen &c came to private view of the Photographic Socy, being the first exhibition in the Refreshment upper room'. (Cole's '&c' embraced the Prince Consort.) The room, the installation and some of the 705 works are shown in Charles Thurston Thompson's photograph (Plate 20). The architectonic layout of the photographs was based on the style of watercolour exhibitions.[11] The startling visual illusion of three-dimensions in stereoscopic photography was becoming very popular. Stereoscopic viewers crowded the tables in the exhibition. Lake Price's *Don Quixote in his Study* (Figure 3) can be picked out in the centre of the display, together with some of the classical busts photographed by Fenton at the British Museum. Highlights of the exhibition included Rejlander's tableau *The Two Ways of Life*, printed from many separate negatives in combination. The full-size composition was offered in the exhibition at 210s. (or 10 guineas), while a 'Small Copy' version was priced at 12s.6d. and individual studies at 7s.6d. each. Equally famous is the portrait by Robert Howlett of the engineer Isambard Kingdom Brunel (Plate 21) and the iron ship he designed, then known as the *Leviathan*, but later renamed *The Great Eastern* (Plate 22). Howlett's coverage of the great ship being built in London's East End is an early example of photojournalism. The photographs originally appeared, translated into wood engravings, in *The Illustrated Times* (16 June 1858).

The Museum's first photographic exhibition was favourably received. 'It is', reported the *Journal of the Photographic Society of London* on 21 January 1858, 'by far

19. Gustave Le Gray (French, 1820–82). **The Great Wave, Sette**, 1856. Albumen print from wet collodion negatives. 13½ × 16¼ in (34.3 × 41.2 cm). C.H. Townshend Bequest, 1868. 68.004.

(right)
Figure 4. Henry Taylor (British, active 1850s–60s). **Bryony (Bryonia dioica)**, *c.*1856. Calotype 6½ × 8 in (16.5 × 20.5 cm). Bought 1857. 36.596.

the best Exhibition the Society has yet collected'. It was the first time that the London society had hosted a full-scale contribution from its French counterpart. Some 250 photographs arrived from Paris. The catalogue lists works by many of the greatest names in French photography, Baldus, Le Gray, Nadar, Nègre, with further contributions from Belgium, Italy and Spain. However, Cole did not repeat his active purchasing of 1856. The only items bought directly from this stunning exhibition were eight photographs by Alinari of drawings in the Uffizi Gallery, Florence. These were bought for 6s.6d. each on 14 September 1858.

The Art Library acquired 600 photographs during 1858, to join its collection of over 8,000 prints, drawings and photographs accumulated by 1859.[12] It acquired, at various times in the 1850s and 1860s, works by Baldus, Nègre and the English master Roger Fenton, whose views of English cathedrals were one of the highlights of the 1858 exhibition. In the same decades, the Museum gained Fenton's photographs of fossils, classical sculpture, Old Master drawings and the skeletons of a man, a gorilla and an emu, taken for the British Museum. Other areas of Fenton's work, such as his photographs from the Crimean War (1854–5) were acquired through the Townshend Bequest in 1868. The first landscapes by Fenton arrived, with some of his finest architectural photographs (Plate 23), as the gift of Miss W.M.A. Brooke in 1935. These are all from the later 1850s and were very probably collected by one of the enthusiasts of photography at that time, in its heyday. Further Fenton landscapes, a unique semi-draped nude, plus portraits, Orientalist tableaux and a Crimean album were acquired at auction in the 1970s and 1980s, as will be related in chapter seven.

Another exhibitor in 1858 was Henry Taylor, who showed close-up landscape details under the general title *Photographic Memoranda from Nature* (Figure 4). The grey tonality of these calotypes suggests that they were printed by chemical development, rather than by sunlight. Taylor may have opted for this method – given the vagaries of English weather – in order to fulfil quotas for editions. His series was published in parts by the photographic dealer H. Hering, from whom the Museum bought them in 1857. Interestingly, they were acquired (as the Art Library's diary of accessions makes clear) through Richard Redgrave himself. Redgrave was not only Art Superintendent but also a Royal Academician. Presumably he acquired Taylor's prints because of their likely benefit to artists, or as valuable aids to students of drawing generally. Thus, the Photography Collection began to take a direction that would be greatly augmented in later decades, as will be shown in chapters four and five.

Painters had, of course, observed the progress of photography with fascination from the beginning. This engrossing topic has been brilliantly discussed by Van Deren Coke in *The Painter and the Photograph* (1964) and Aaron Scharf in *Art and Photography* (1968). Even the busy MP William Ewart referred to it in a letter as early as 1850: 'If I am not mistaken, some artists are using the Photographic or Daguerreotype process for light and shade. This is painting through the agency of the sun. I think this discovery will make a revolution in art. But it is only my opinion...'[13] A few years later the amateur's suspicion had become the professional's fact: 'An artist looking at a photographic picture may learn some of the mysteries of light and shadow, which cannot be arrived at by any other study: and photography, so used, is of immense advantage to art... Until of late, a tree was any tree; but now-a-days a tree must be unmistakably an oak, an ash, an elm, or of whatever kind it pretends to be; for these same sun-pictures have taught thousands to study the minute details of a great whole, who never gave the subject a passing thought before'.[14]

The South Kensington exhibition contained 'innumerable studies of foreground subjects invaluable to the artist. The greatest triumph of photography is with subjects like these, which are near, upon one plane, and full of minute character – her truthfulness of record is in such cases quite miraculous'. These last remarks are from an article in the *Daily News* on 23 February 1858. Under the heading 'FINE ARTS – EXHIBITION OF THE PHOTOGRAPHIC SOCIETY', the 1858 exhibition was acclaimed as the society's 'great public display of the season'.

On 13 March 1858 a glittering soirée was held at the South Kensington Museum by the Council of the Photographic Society. 'A great part of the Museum, and the

20. CHARLES THURSTON THOMPSON (British, 1816–68). **Exhibition of the Photographic Society of London and the Société française de photographie at the South Kensington Museum**, 1858. Albumen print from wet collodion negative. 11⅜ × 13⅛ in (29 × 33.5 cm). Given by Alan S. Cole, 1913. 2715–1913.

large Board Room (which was turned into a refreshment-room) was also lighted up and thrown open for the occasion'.[15] As previously mentioned, although the exhibition was much admired, none of the great photographs on display was bought by the Museum. Le Gray's *Great Wave* was exhibited but not acquired at the time – at least, not by the Museum. Fortunately many fine French photographs of the 1850s, including works by Giroux and Le Gray (Plates 18 and 19), and Camille Silvy's celebrated *River Scene, France* (1858),[16] were acquired by a prescient collector.

Chauncy Hare Townshend (1798–1868) was a poet, a priest (non-practising), a mesmerist, a noted art collector, an intimate friend of Dickens and – perhaps most important – a millionaire. Townshend's splendid library and collection of Old Masters, modern paintings, prints, watercolours, fossils, coins, casts, intaglios and precious stones were housed in a beautiful, balconied house in London's Park Lane. 'Every house in which he lived', wrote a contemporary, 'had, indeed, the interest of an art museum'.[17] Like Henry Cole, Townshend had visited the 1855 Paris Exposition. Perhaps he noticed the photographs by Giroux and Le Gray there?

From the middle of the 1850s there was a serious trade in fine photographs and Townshend could have acquired his exquisite collection from a number of dealers in London and Paris. The firm of Murray & Heath, for example, sold contemporary French work, in a central London location at 43 Piccadilly. There were many places to buy fine photographs during this decade, in which the medium became more fashionable from year to year. In 1858 a correspondent wrote to the *Journal of the Photographic Society* asking for more thorough coverage of new photography, for the benefit of 'those making collections'. There was much on offer: 'I myself never pass such shops as Murray and Heath's and Fore's of Piccadilly, Hogarth's of the Haymarket, or Spooner's in the Strand, and many others that I could name, without receiving a great deal of pleasure and instruction in the truly beautiful art'.[18]

No documents survive to tell us about sales from the 1858 exhibition in South Kensington. However, a unique and abundant collection of correspondence has fortunately been preserved from the annual exhibition of the Photographic Society of Scotland in Edinburgh, later in the same year. This shows that exhibitions were marketing opportunities. Many prints were sold (the Society taking 10 per cent commission). A well known photographer could expect to sell a dozen prints; Henry Peach Robinson sold his by the score.[19]

'Theta', an engaging pseudonymous photography critic, wrote about the keen photography collectors of the 1850s:

> The invisible spirit of the sun, some time since turned artist, is beginning to make a figure in his profession; whether he will ever get into the Academy is quite another matter; however, thank goodness! an artist may be A1 and yet not R.A... Photography revels in light; the old art was a black art... Sunlight is the

21. ROBERT HOWLETT (British, 1831–58). **Isambard Kingdom Brunel and Launching Chains of *The Great Eastern***, 1857. Albumen print from wet collodion negative. 11¼ × 9⅛ in (28.5 × 23.2 cm). Bought 1979. Ph.246–1979.

22. Robert Howlett (British, 1831–58). ***The Great Eastern* under Construction**, 1857. Albumen print from wet collodion negative. 11¼ × 14¼ in (28.5 × 36 cm). Bought 1979. Ph.258–1979.

> Londoner's ideal; he lives too much in the old masters' brown murkiness, to wish to see it eternally reproduced on canvas; so when the photographs came, with their rich expanses of sun and shade, the Londoner at once began to buy these plots of eternal sunshine, and to light his murky halls then and there with the said plots of ungilt sunshine.[20]

Townshend certainly owned Old Master paintings and spacious halls, perhaps even murky ones, if we can trust Dickens's portrait of him as 'Cousin Feenix' in *Dombey and Son*.[21]

So much of the intimate early history of the South Kensington Museum can never be reconstructed. However, one can still eavesdrop on a conversation in the corridors in its early years. One of the curators, G.F. Duncombe, recalled walking through the Museum with the Rev. Townshend. The collector, an old friend of Duncombe's family, stopped to examine the jewels exhibited in the Museum's South Court, to compare them with those in his own collection. Duncombe wrote later of the turn their conversation took:

> Mr Townshend having no children, it occurred to me that it would be a noble thing for him to leave his collection by will to the South Kensington Museum, which at that time had no precious stones except on loan. I made the suggestion to him and he seemed pleased with the idea, and subsequently often referred to it.[22]

On Townshend's death in 1868 his will gave the choice of his collections to the Museum. Any pictures or books not wanted were to go to a local museum in Wisbech, Cambridgeshire, near Townshend's country estates. Two officials from South Kensington – 'JC' (presumably Joseph Cundall, photographer and antiquarian, who took charge of the Museum's photographic service after the premature death of Thurston Thompson) and 'RR' (Richard Redgrave) – went through the contents of the treasure house. Each initialled items from the inventory for acceptance. JC marked all the photographs by Le Gray, Giroux and others. There were 31 'various' and 47 of buildings. Townshend kept them, museum-style, in portfolios in a press. The Le Grays are considered today to be among the very finest selections of his surviving prints in the world. This reflects well on Townshend's discrimination as a connoisseur and his care as a collector. Because the prints were scrupulously printed and gold-toned in the first place, and have always been kept in museum conditions, they have remained pristine.

Although the installation was admired and emulated, the first ever international exhibition of photography at the South Kensington Museum was not considered a success. Perhaps some were put off by the admission fee of one shilling, though this was standard for the Photographic Society's shows (five shillings would buy a season ticket). But the problem was more fundamental. South Kensington, about two miles from Piccadilly Circus, was simply too far out of London. 'We must say', declared the *Journal of the Photographic Society* on 21 May 1858, 'that a more out-of-the-way place could not well have been chosen. It would be a very curious calculation to know how many of the few who visited that really admirable exhibition, went there for the sake of the photographs themselves – pilgrims to the shrine of photography – as distinguished from those visitors who made a "day out" of it, and "did" the Kensington Museum at the same time.' Although South Kensington seemed out-of-the-way to some Londoners, attendances were remarkably high: 456,288 visitors in 1858.[23] The Museum was already becoming an institution of global significance, as we shall see in the next chapter.

23. ROGER FENTON (British, 1819–69). **Roslyn Chapel**, 1856. Salted paper print from wet collodion negative. Inscribed in ink H.40 and signed. 13 13/16 × 16 11/16 in (35.1 × 42.4 cm). Given by Miss W.M.A Brooke, 1935. 290–1935

No 45. Spokan Indians.

CHAPTER THREE

All the World under the Subjugation of Art

Henry Cole sent the Photographic Society's 1860 exhibition catalogue to J.C. Robinson, Curator of the Museum's art collections: 'Mr Robinson – To see if anything should be bought'. Unsurprisingly, nothing was. Robinson was usually hunting the biggest game in the art world: a room from a Renaissance palace, a complete Italian fountain or the collection of a connoisseur. Under Cole's direction, Robinson led the most ambitiously acquisitive phase in the Museum's history. This focused chiefly on European Medieval and Renaissance decorative arts and sculpture. He established not only the Museum's core collections, but also its tradition of connoisseurship. The original works of art, architecture and design were complemented by the requirements of education and research: plaster casts, electrotypes, books, prints of many kinds and, above all, photographs.

Although Robinson had no interest in photography as art, he took the strongest interest in photographs *of* art. He, Cole and Redgrave constantly acquired photographs for the collection from London dealers or during their travels in Europe. Robinson briefed Charles Thurston Thompson before he set out for north-west Spain to photograph the pilgrimage church of Santiago de Compostela in 1866.[1] The shooting script is exhaustive and exact. Few photographers can ever have been so thoroughly briefed. Robinson asked Thurston Thompson to take a general view of the cathedral and its adjoining buildings from high ground nearby, called the Campo de Estrella. He was to photograph, 'from betwixt the 9th and 10th tree at the roadside'. Then he was to photograph 'from betwixt two of the old oak trees higher up the road – there is an opening in the screen of trees where the right point of view will be easily found'.[2] The list runs to 50 paragraphs and names many individual items, including the 'Silver suspended lamps in front of [the] high altar'. The Museum was simultaneously having a plaster cast made, by Brucciani of London, of the cathedral's Porticó de la Gloria. This is still a major feature of the Cast Courts at the Victoria and Albert Museum today. These ambitious undertakings are typical of the Museum's vigorous attempts to comprehend the world in images.

A set of Thurston Thompson's photographs from this campaign was published by the Arundel Society in 1868. The society was named after Thomas Howard, 2nd Earl of Arundel (1589–1646), 'the father of Vertu [love of and taste for the fine arts] in England'.[3] Between 1848 and 1897 it produced numerous volumes of reproductions of works of art, often using photography. For many years the society had its own sales area in the South Kensington Museum.

24. Royal Engineers US/Canada Border Survey. **Spokan Indians**, 1860–1. Albumen print. 5¼ × 5⅜ in (13 × 13.5 cm). Received from the Foreign Office, 1863. 40.007.

Robinson was not only one of the first art historians, but also one of the first to use photographs to inform connoisseurship.[4] In 1870 he published *A Critical Account of the Drawings by Michel Angelo and Rafaello in the University Galleries, Oxford*. He wrote in the introduction that 'photography has in our own time effected an entire revolution: the drawings of the ancient masters may now be multiplied virtually without limit: and thus, what was before a practical impossibility, namely, the actual comparison of the numerous dispersed drawings of any particular master, has become quite practicable'. His catalogue was saluted by Francis Haskell in 1980 as 'perhaps the single most important contribution to scholarly connoisseurship made by an Englishman in the nineteenth-century'.[5]

The South Kensington Museum became a world-class repository and a global influence. 'South Kensington was consistently the referenced model for the rhetoric behind virtually every American art museum founded in the 1870s', writes Michael Conforti, adding that the Metropolitan Museum of Art, in New York, began on South Kensington lines.[6] By 1875 the Metropolitan was 'exhibiting "repros of works of art in [the] South Kensington Museum" on the ground floor of its temporary quarters'.

Photography was well set to participate in the imperial years of both Britain and South Kensington. By the mid-1850s the wet collodion process had achieved ascendancy and photographic materials had become generally standardized. No longer a matter of home-made recipes exchanged among friends, photographic supplies were available ready-made and world-wide. Photographic procedures were established enough to be easily taught and learned.

The 1858 exhibition at the South Kensington Museum, discussed in the last chapter, included – for the first time – a display of photographs by soldiers of the Royal Engineers. This included 'A Series of Photographs illustrating the application of Photography to the reduction of Maps, as introduced by Colonel James, Royal Engineers, and practised in the Ordnance Survey under his direction.' The catalogue entry added: 'N.B. By this process there is an annual saving of [*sic*] the country of £1800'. Soldier-photographers of the Royal Engineers exhibited photographs taken in St Petersburg, Moscow and Singapore. The *Journal of the Photographic Society* of 21 July 1858 commented: 'in a few years time there will be photographic stations spread all over the world, and having their results recorded in the War Department; and in a short time all the world will be brought under the subjugation of Art'.

There was a long-standing connection between South Kensington and the Royal Engineers. Two companies had undertaken security and other duties at the Great Exhibition. Cole managed to retain the connection with the sappers, who served as firemen, warders and general help in his new institution. In 1856 Charles Thurston Thompson was appointed by the War Department to teach photography to non-commissioned officers of the Royal Engineers, and the corps was probably the first military unit to learn photography under a formalized system of instruction. From

25. Royal Engineers US/Canada Border Survey. **Columbia River Salmon Caught at Kettle Falls**, 1860–1. Albumen print. 4¼ × 8¾ in (11 × 22.5 cm). Received from the Foreign Office, 1863. 40.081.

No. 49. Columbia River Salmon
caught at Kettle Falls.

Figure 5. ROGER FENTON (British, 1819–69). **Photographic Van**, 1854. Salted paper print from wet collodion negative. 6¾ × 6½ in (17.3 x 16.5 cm). Bought 1979. Ph. 263–1979.

1857 Thurston Thompson was paid ten guineas when each soldier was granted a certificate of proficiency – signed by Henry Cole.[7] Soldier-photographers trained in South Kensington travelled on assignment to Africa, India, China and Central and North America.

In 1863 a portfolio of 81 photographs was transferred from the Foreign Office to the South Kensington Museum. Taken for the British Boundary Commission, they documented the US/Canada Border Survey, from the crest of the Rockies westwards along the 49th Parallel to the coast. A gold rush to British Columbia in the late 1850s hastened the need to complete the work of the Boundary Commission, which began in 1857. The border itself was surveyed, cut and marked with cairns by sappers of the Royal Engineers. The anonymous soldier-photographers in the party produced, in 1860–1, 'the earliest significant body of photographs made in the Pacific Northwest'.[8]

The photographers captioned their images with care, but left no other records. Fortunately, John Keast Lord, a naturalist with the party, published his reminiscences in 1866. Many of the photographs were taken in the vicinity of Fort Colville, in American territory, between the Rockies and the Cascade Mountains, where the Hudson's Bay Company's principal trading post was located. Lord wrote of the flora and fauna of the place, and of a salmon leap at Kettle Falls on the Columbia River, where the waters bubbled and boiled. He wrote: 'The Indians at first steadily refused to allow the photographer and his machine to come near the falls, declaring it a box of bad "medicine" that would surely drive every salmon away; and not until an old Romish priest who was at the trading post explained it to them, did they permit a photograph to be taken'.[9] Although perhaps only an expert fisherman could estimate its actual size, the portrait of the Kettle Falls salmon seems straightforward (Plate 25). However, as we shall see, one should not expect early documentary photographs to be any less manipulated than television documentaries are today.

Lord could not, of course, publish the photographs in his book in their original form. They had to be copied by a wood engraver and printed from blocks. The ability to print convincing photographic images simultaneously with text was still in the future – and will be discussed in the next chapter. Lord's book carried a wood engraving of the photograph shown in Plate 24: 'The illustration in which there are three figures represents three Spokan Indians; one, the figure to the left, has a stone celt [prehistoric chisel or axe head made of stone, bronze or occasionally iron], which I obtained; it is now in the British Museum collection, and deemed the finest specimen they possess. There is no record of how it became his property, all that I could glean respecting its history was that for a long period it had been handed down from father to son as a valuable heirloom; hereditary inheritance I find with Indians, as with whites, is weak to resist the all-potent dollar. The centre figure holds a rifle, which was not his own, but borrowed from Macdonald, the chief trader, for the occasion. The figure on the right has a bow and arrow, both of which were also purchased'.[10]

This suggests that the photograph was quite a production, in which actuality was improved, if that is the word, by some or all of the participants. However, is the written word any more trustworthy than the photographic 'document'? Consultation with the British Museum in 1996 elicited the surprising information that Lord had not given them a celt.[11] He did give a bladed tool which can be seen in the photograph (held by the Indian at the left). The object's nineteenth-century label, presumably based on information from the donor, states grandly, if somewhat vaguely, that it had been found 'in the Gravel of British Columbia' – but perhaps it was really bought from the Indian holding it in the photograph, in Eastern Washington State.

The Canadian historian Joan M. Schwartz reminds us that the bulky equipment of the wet-plate era influenced the range of subjects recorded: 'Although pack horse and cart could negotiate crude trails, dense vegetation and rugged terrain rendered much of the Coast and Interior inaccessible to itinerant professional photographers burdened by portable darkrooms, heavy equipment and copious supplies... The deliberation and effort entailed by each exposure made collodion photography anything but a spontaneous procedure and nineteenth century photographs anything but haphazard compositions'.[12] Roger Fenton's view of his 'Photographic Van' in the Crimea indicates something of the scale of a travelling photographer's operation (Figure 5).

26. Royal Engineers US/Canada Border Commission. **Guard House, US Post, Lower Cascades, Right Bank of Columbia River**, 1860–1. Albumen print. 7⅝ × 11 in (19.5 × 28 cm). Received from the Foreign Office, 1863. 40.042.

So when the unknown sappers photographed a United States guard house in the Lower Cascades (Plate 26), it could have taken an hour or more to set up the camera and to hand-coat the glass plate with collodion. Their view of the outpost, with its blanket-hung railings, modest cairn and single field-gun, is set in just the right amount of space to suggest that this is a lonely, dangerous spot. The image persuades us, perhaps, of the value of the 'arbitrary' photographic rectangle. Forced to conjecture, we therefore imagine. The place was dangerous, of course, to the unseen native inhabitants as well as to the invisible garrison. It was a place of military discipline, in which the precise position of an artillery-piece was partly ceremonial and partly, perhaps – in the hundreds of miles of surrounding silence – bravado. Or was this gun, too, positioned for the photograph?

On the other side of the world, the Australian Algernon Hall also placed his tripod with care to make the views illustrated here (Plates 27–8). He was the town photographer of Beechworth, 160 miles from Melbourne, the capital of Victoria (then a 'colony', not yet a state). Victoria had acquired independence from New South Wales only in 1851, five years before Hall set up his shingle. He presumably came to Beechworth because it needed portraits – both Victoria and the town grew at an astonishing speed during the gold-rush of the 1850s. Many of his portraits were commissioned, no doubt, by miners and sent to parents and loved ones. His portrait of Beechworth itself shows the town at its dapper best. The recent researches of Joanne Delzoppo have shown that in 1866 Hall was paid £10 by Beechworth's Council to produce fourteen views. These were to be exhibited at the 1866 Intercolonial Exhibition and after that at the Paris International Exhibition, the following year.[13]

The young settlement boasted a population of 2,500 in 1866. Hall photographed the court house, hospital, town hall, the churches, schools, hotels, banks, main streets and goldfields. He made the community seem as clear and comprehensible as a toy town. Using a magnifying glass, as Talbot suggested, we can note that the amenities included regular deliveries of *The Australasian* newspaper, with its 'English Mail News', and that J. Ingram was not only a Seedsman, Bookseller and Stationer, but

No 10. Guard House, &c at Post Lower Cascades.
Right bank of Columbia River.

27. Algernon Hall (Australian, active 1856–1901). **Ford Street, East Side, Beechworth, Australia**, 1866.
Albumen print. 8 × 9¾ in (20 × 24.5 cm). Given by the Borough of Beechworth, 1867. 56.189.

28. ALGERNON HALL (Australian, active 1856–1901). **Post Office, Camp Street, Beechworth, Australia**, 1866. Albumen print. 8 × 9¾ in (20 × 24.5 cm). Given by the Borough of Beechworth, 1867. 56.190.

also a Florist. In the event, Hall's photographs of the town and surrounding areas were not shown at the Paris exhibition.

They were sent by the Shire of Beechworth Council to the South Kensington Museum in 1867. A Mr Deutschware undertook to deliver them personally and they were accompanied by a short history of Beechworth's equally short history, ceremonially scribed. The South Kensington Museum was a major organizer of the Paris exhibition, and thus a suitable recipient of the photographs. Presumably, South Kensington's fame had also spread through the press. Its influence was already felt nearby. Melbourne's new Museum of Art (now the National Gallery of Victoria) opened in 1859 with the South Kensington mix of casts, photographs and education. Through Hall's cogent photographs, Beechworth presented itself internationally as a civic success.

Spinning the globe again, Captain Linnaeus Tripe (1822–1902) of the 12th Madras Native Infantry also had a connection with South Kensington. He photographed in 1857–9 for the Madras Presidency, home of the new Madras School of Industrial Arts. Tripe was appointed to photograph particularly 'edifices, sculptures and inscriptions of much beauty or interest both historical and artistic'.[14] Dr Alexander Hunter, founder of the school, was responsible for sending Tripe's work to South Kensington. There are large groups of his photographs in the National Art Library (bound volumes), the Indian and South East Asian Department and the Photography Collection. No doubt because of their convenience (compared to glass), Tripe used paper negatives on his photographic expeditions. Janet Dewan has emphasized that Tripe 'interpreted his mandate to include "any object with which people, at a distance, can only become acquainted by means of a representation"'.[15] Plate 29 represents the most notable Muslim monument in Trichinopoly. The mosque, formerly a Hindu temple, contains the tomb of Sultan Saiyad Babayya Nathar Shah, a Muslim saint (called Nuttur Auleah in Tripe's title). However, the shrine is shown in a context of simple dwellings, perhaps for pilgrims, and the carefully nurtured pot-plants of residents. Tripe was interested in portraying the spirit of place as well as spiritual places.

The characteristic grain and informality of Tripe's photographs, and their rich purple colour, contrast with the crystal clarity of the prints produced in the following decade by Samuel Bourne (1834–1912). Using the wet collodion process, Bourne photographed such monuments as the Taj Mahal, already a site of great fascination for the British (Plate 30). He contrived the composition, and arranged its staffage, so that the viewer's eye reaches from Akbar's fort to the Taj Mahal, built by his grandson Shah Jahan. Many of the Anglo-Indians to whom he sold the photograph would have known that Shah Jahan had been incarcerated at the fort for much of his later life, and that the former emperor gazed from imprisonment at the white marble building he had raised in memory of his wife, beside the Jumna.

29. LINNAEUS TRIPE (British, 1822–1902). **Musjid of Nuttur Auleah, Trichinopoly, India**, 1858. Salted paper print (lightly albumenised?) from paper negative. 10¾ × 15⅛ in (27.2 × 38.3 cm). Received from Dr Hunter, Madras School of Art, 1862. 33.801.

Agra.
53.243.
Bourne 1222

30. Samuel Bourne (British, 1834–1912). **Agra: The Fort, the Palace of Akbar, with Taj in the Distance**, *c.*1865. Albumen print from wet collodion negative. 9¼ × 11¾ in (23.7 × 29.8 cm). Bought from Bourne and Shepherd, Simla, 1867. 53.243.

Bourne and his partner Charles Shepherd shrewdly based their studio at Simla, the hill station north of Delhi which served as the summer capital of the Raj. In 1866 the company sent its first catalogue to South Kensington. The Museum bought all of the 668 photographs listed for £205.16s.9d. These photographs are now divided between the Photography Collection and the Indian and South East Asian Department.

This major acquisition may have been prompted by James Fergusson (1808–86), a Western scholar who pioneered the study of Indian monuments and had been associated with Cole's Department from the beginning. Fergusson remarked, in a lecture at the Society of Arts on 19 December 1866, that Western knowledge of Indian architecture had long been confined to a limited circle. Publications using earlier methods of illustration had proved 'cumbrous and expensive... and no general interest in the subject is diffused among the public at large'.[16] However, now 'new sets of Photographs are constantly being sent home from India. Almost all the best-known buildings have been taken... and any one, at a small expense, may now make himself master of any branch of the inquiry... I have learnt as much, if not more, of Indian Architecture during the last two or three years than I did during my residence in India...' The point of studying Indian architecture was not, Fergusson added, to allow Western architects to produce pastiche – 'I must consider copying the Indian styles as a crime' – but to study underlying principles, widening 'the base of our observation, and so enabling students to realise the true definition of the art, for till that is grasped there seems little hope of any improvement in our architecture'.

Henry Cole led the discussion following Fergusson's lecture. He recalled the superiority of Indian textiles over their European counterparts at the Great Exhibition and feared that 'the Schools of Design lately established in Calcutta, Madras, and Bombay, instead of leading the natives to advance in their own styles, should create a hybrid style, the most detestable ever seen'. The West, he argued, had 'a great deal more to learn from the Indians than we could hope to teach them in the designing of patterns'.[17] Returning to the question of photography, Cole 'hoped some plan would be arranged by which we might have in this country a systematic collection of photographs of Indian buildings; there were already skilful photographers high up in the hills in India, who were in possession of thousands of these photographs, and he hoped we should soon see them in this country'. Cole was well informed. His elder son, H.H. Cole, was already working in India, photographing monuments and organizing plaster casts.

Fergusson himself masterminded a display on Indian architecture at the International Exhibition in Paris the following year. He showed the Elliott marbles, plaster casts, and photographs by Bourne and Shepherd. A contemporary report described these as 'the rare and costly collection of photographs of Indian buildings' and summed up their contribution to the 1867 International Exhibition: 'It is doubtful whether England ever sent to that gathering of the world's best any other series which so strongly engaged the interest of continental scholars'.[18] The photographs were also shown in South Kensington's own Oriental Court and some were published, as reduced copies, in *Illustrations of Various Styles of Indian Architecture*, issued by the Museum in 1869.[19]

Samuel Bourne, the most polished photographer of the jewel in Britain's imperial crown, has recently been both carefully probed for imperialism and, understandably, summarily convicted of it.[20] Bourne's photography was certainly imperial, his market very largely Anglo-Indian (although the studio's work was commercially distributed in London and Paris, as well as Bombay, Calcutta and Simla) and he is unlikely to have disapproved of the empire. However, it is surely true that he photographed India sympathetically and with skill – and that he shaped the image of India in the West more than any photographer prior to Henri Cartier-Bresson in the 1940s.

Naked imperialism of a different kind appears in Plate 31. This is the work of Charles Clifford (*c.*1820–63), another British photographer who established himself overseas and made views of his adopted country; his photographs are surely the finest ever made of Spanish architecture. Clifford and his wife Jane, also a photographer, based themselves in Madrid in 1852 and worked under the patronage of Queen Isabella II. He used both paper and glass negatives to make large-scale photographs of Spanish cities and the principal monuments. Perhaps because of J.C. Robinson's special interest in Spanish art, the Museum acquired 296 Clifford photographs in the 1850s and 1860s.

Clifford's photograph of the Torre del Vino in Granada is a memorable rendition of the building's surfaces and style. A variant view of this building took the fancy of Roland Barthes in his *Camera Lucida* (1982). Barthes mused on the kinds of longing engendered by photographs. His desire to live in this building was neither, he reflected, a matter of consumerism nor an exercise in power. Nonetheless, 'I want to live there – *en finesse*'.[21] With characteristic vigour, however, Clifford had photographed the wine tower from both sides and the image in Plate 31 is in striking contrast to the one that entranced Barthes. Through the Moorish gateway juts the corner of a very different structure. As Lee Fontanella has recently noted, Clifford's photograph illustrates with perfect clarity how the Holy Roman Emperor Charles V (1500–58), who reigned as Charles I of Spain, deliberately sited his Renaissance palaces in the midst of Muslim areas as demonstrations of imperial power.[22]

Even larger – mammoth plate – photographs were produced in Paris and London in the 1850s and 1860s. Edouard Baldus made spectacular (28½ × 21 in, 72.5 × 53 cm) views of the new buildings of the Louvre commissioned by Napoleon III. Four of these superb pieces were shown in South Kensington at the 1858 exhibition and acquired ten years later. Comparable views were made at Westminster by Stephen Ayling (Plate 32). Ayling, a commercial photographer with premises in New

31. CHARLES CLIFFORD (British, *c.*1820–63). **Torre del Vino, Granada**, *c.*1860. Albumen print. 16½ × 12 in (42 × 30.5 cm). Bought 1866. 47.789.

32. Stephen Ayling (British, active 1860–72). **Westminster Henry VII Chapel Exterior and Westminster Hall**, 1867. Albumen print. 16¼ × 21¾ in (41.5 × 55.5 cm). Bought 1868. 61.116.

Oxford Street from 1860–70, showed his large views at a soirée at the Photographic Society on 16 November 1867. He sold three views of Westminster to the Museum in the following year.

The photographs were taken with a camera of impressive size, but Ayling manoeuvred his equipment into position so accurately that Plate 32 shows us two buildings almost as if they were one. He evidently wanted to demonstrate how the forms of the nearer building are echoed by those of the further. The nearer is Henry VII's Chapel, part of Westminster Abbey, and built in the early sixteenth century. The further building is the Palace of Westminster, home of the Houses of Parliament, designed by Charles Barry and A.W.N. Pugin from 1835 and built over the succeeding three decades. Both buildings are in the Perpendicular Gothic style. Ayling shows how faithfully, but far from slavishly, Pugin faced Barry's new structure to harmonize with its great neighbour. The finials dance, inventively modified, from the old structure to the new: 'contextual architecture' *par excellence*. Few can have known Pugin's work better than Ayling when he made these views in 1867. He had published *Photographs from Sketches by A.W.N. Pugin* in two volumes in 1865. His photograph of the ancient and modern Gothic structures compresses the space between them. This was no mean illusion, as the distance is ample for the four-lane highway that runs between the buildings today.

Although 'pointed Gothic' had powerful advocates as the style for public buildings in the 1850s and 1860s,[23] Henry Cole chose differently for South Kensington. He favoured Renaissance Italy. Here, too, photography played a part. Cole visited Rome in 1858–9 and was particularly taken with the cloisters of the church of San Giovanni in Laterano.[24] It was then that he acquired a superb set of photographs of his favourite Roman places. Fifty years later, in 1906, his younger son, Alan S. Cole, gave the Museum 34 'Mounted photographs of various buildings in Rome taken at Mr. Cole's direction – in preparation for the buildings to be erected for the South Kensington Museum and South Kensington Estate'.[25] These included the cloisters of the Lateran church and the gardens of the Corsini palace. The Roman flavour of the buildings put up in South Kensington, especially those around the Museum's garden, is neither accidental nor unspecific. Cole's architect, Francis Fowke, adopted the delicate coupled columns of San Giovanni in Laterano: spiral columns support semi-circular arches grouped together to form open arcades. Photography had taken over the important business of describing the substance of stone and the intricacy of ornament. Henry Cole began the Museum's extraordinary collection of architectural photography to inform and inspire the planners, architects and builders of his own and later times. In the 1860s Cole collected further interesting photographs, by Julia Margaret Cameron, arguably to inform and inspire designers, as we shall see in the next chapter.

CHAPTER FOUR

A Fine Art and a Manufacturing Art

In the ten years after 1851 photography became an industry – 'a household word and a household want', as Lady Eastlake wrote in 1857, '... used alike by art and science, by love, business, and justice'.[1] The Census of 1851 listed 51 professional photographers. The 1861 Census recorded 2,534. Photography was suddenly everywhere and doing everything. The growing industrialization of the medium led to a continuing crisis of identity. Debates and schisms ran through the nineteenth century, and continued into the next. Amateur or professional, art or science, fine art or manufacturing technology? It was even argued that exposing the negative was one thing and printing from it something quite different. On the eve of the second annual exhibition of the Photographic Society of London, and of the Paris Exhibition of 1855, an editorial in the society's journal stated that:

> Photography is undoubtedly to be regarded as a Fine Art, in reference to the production of the original impressions obtained in the camera. Taste, acquaintance with the pictorial value of natural effects, and an eye educated in the observation of the Picturesque, the beautiful and the sublime in nature, are requisites in the true photographic artist, as in the painter. But the printing of positives from the negatives, where skilful mechanical manipulation is the chief agent, falls under the class of the Manufacturing Arts, and shares one advantage which these possess, – the capability of indefinite multiplication and wide diffusion of their products.[2]

Indeed, some photographers like Charles Thurston Thompson only made negatives – he left the printing to his staff.[3] Leading amateurs in the 1850s were also happy to have professionals do their printing to fill orders from exhibitions.[4] The last sentence in the passage quoted above refers particularly to the advantageous fact that photographers could show the same works simultaneously in both London and Paris.

Paris took the bold step of inaugurating the first 'Salon' of photography as a fine art, alongside the biennial Salon des Beaux-Arts in 1859. However, almost simultaneously, photography went into mass-production. The Parisian photographer A.A.E. Disderi revolutionized the portrait business. 'Cartes de visite' or 'album' portraits were low-cost miniatures. Six or eight portraits, allowing three or four different poses, could be recorded on one glass negative. There were several variations on the procedure, but they were all means of achieving high volume at low cost.

33. Camille Silvy (French, 1834–1910). **Flora Bradford**, 15 March 1860. Albumen print proof sheet from wet collodion negative. 8 × 10 in (20.3 × 25.4 cm). E.1027–1992.

Plate 33 is by the Frenchman, Camille Silvy, who – at the age of 25 – brought the technique to London in the summer of 1859. He set up not only a fashionable studio, beside Hyde Park in Bayswater, but also, in the yard at the back, a model Victorian factory engaged in the mass-production of portrait photographs.[4] Silvy employed a staff of forty. He usually photographed three poses (each pose twice) per plate. Here Silvy, arguably the best in the business in London or Paris, was working with his favourite subject – a beautifully dressed young woman, and playing with mirror reflections. The chosen image was then cut out, mounted on card and supplied by the dozen, the score or the hundred. Such portraits, plus those of royalty and other celebrities (which were published by the hundred thousand and more) were circulated and exchanged at many levels of society during the cartes mania of the early 1860s.

Cartes were ubiquitous, and often preposterous, studio confections. The pompousness of these Lilliputian portraits was to receive a spirited come-uppance at the hands, and scissors, of the collagiste whose montages are shown in Plate 34 and Figure 6. They are from an album compiled in the 1860s, and later, which belonged to Kate E. Gough. Marina Warner has described the special wit and fantasy of this album:

> If Kate Gough created these images, she deserves to enter the history of Surrealism. Her mixed media treatment of family snaps has a wild wit that prefigures the collage novels of Max Ernst half a century later; they catch the tonic irreverent tone of her contemporary, Lewis Carroll. At the height of the controversy over Darwinism, she inserts family portraits into a sketch of monkeys in a tree [Figure 6]; single ladies in hats are transformed into ducks, gliding in stately fashion among reeds; a man's head comes up in a bucket from a well; a cricket team floats in a chinoiserie watercolour of a lotus with carp below. The dislocations of scale (babies in convolvulus trumpets), the mixture of farce and solemnity, the jeux d'esprit in fantastic vein (touches of fairlylore in the children mounted on swallows and nesting in flowers) all anticipate the deflationary devices of the Surrealists.[5]

34. Attributed to KATE E. GOUGH (British, active 1860s–80s). Photograph album with painted borders and decoration, stamped K.E.G on front cover. Untitled [ducks], *c.*1870. Albumen prints and watercolour. 9 × 6½ in (22.9 × 16.5 cm). Given by Guy Eardley-Wilmot, 1963. 872–1963.

(left)
Figure 6. Attributed to KATE E. GOUGH (British, active 1860s–80s). Untitled [monkeys in a tree]. Albumen prints and watercolour. 7⅞ × 5⅞ in (20 × 15 cm). Given by Guy Eardley-Wilmot, 1963. 865–1963.

35. CLEMENTINA, VISCOUNTESS HAWARDEN (British, 1822–65). **Study from Life**, *c.*1860. Albumen print. 9¼ × 9¾ in (23.5 × 24.8 cm). Given by Lady Clementina Tottenham, 1939. 267– 1947.

(right)
Figure 7. Attributed to KATE E. GOUGH (British, active 1860s–80s). Untitled [double self-portrait], *c.*1880. Albumen prints and watercolour. 14 x 10 in (35.5 x 25.4 cm). Given by Guy Eardley-Wilmot, 1963. 855–1963.

Possibly the double portrait in Figure 7, the most modern image of all, is the artist herself and a play on the multiplicity of the photograph. This seems the likeliest identification, although Kate Gough (maiden name Rolls Hoare) had a twin sister, with whom she was painted by Sir John Millais in 1876.[6] Referring to the well worn association of photography with death, Marina Warner concludes that an album like this, on the contrary, 'acts less as an index of decay than as a voice raised against banality'.

The photographs of Clementina, Lady Hawarden also speak against commercial banality (although not in a raised voice) and in favour of experiment. Her oeuvre of some 800 photographs was chiefly conceived in the South Kensington milieu in the late 1850s and early 1860s. She was the daughter of Admiral the Hon. Elphinstone Fleeming and his Spanish wife, Catalina Paulina Alessandro. In 1845 she married Cornwallis Maude, who succeeded to the title of Viscount Hawarden, and to the family estate in Dundrum, Co. Tipperary, in 1856. Virginia Dodier, who has compiled an invaluable catalogue raisonné of Lady Hawarden's oeuvre, believes that she began to photograph about 1857. In 1859 the Hawardens settled in a newly built house in Prince's Gate, less than five minutes walk from South Kensington. Lady Hawarden had connexions with the Museum. Did she see the 1858 exhibition? It included a portrait of her husband (by Robert C. May) and works which may have provided the starting point for her own exploratory 'Studies from life' – namely, O. G. Rejlander's 'Studies' for his large composite photograph 'Two Ways of Life'.

In June 1864 Lady Hawarden took part in a Grand Fête and Bazaar held in South Kensington's Horticultural Gardens. Other participants included Henry Cole and Charles Thurston Thompson. They were raising funds to build a new studio on the roof of the Female School of Art in Queen's Square (of which Cole's wife Marian had been a 'Lady Visitor' in 1863). Lady Hawarden ran a stall with Thurston Thompson, taking portraits and selling her own prints in aid of the art school. Marian Cole's album, already referred to, includes several of Lady Hawarden's photographs, perhaps acquired on this occasion. Another talented amateur, Lewis Carroll, visited the fête, met Lady Hawarden and arranged for her to photograph his young friends Mary and Irene MacDonald. The five photographs that he acquired are now in the Gernsheim Collection at the University of Texas. In 1863 and 1864 Lady Hawarden was awarded prize medals at the Photographic Society's exhibitions. 'Should [her] studies be published,' wrote the *Photographic News* in 1863, 'we should recommend every portrait photographer to possess and study them'.[7]

In the same year Jabez Hogg, one of the earliest and best portrait photographers, published a generous 'Tribute to Amateurs':

> Though the extensive diffusion and numerous applications of the art depend upon the professional, yet it must be always borne in mind that the original discoveries – marked improvements – are made by the amateur... It is scarcely to be wondered at that the impulses forward should emanate rather from the amateur than the professional. The former pursues the art for pleasure, the latter for profit. The one can try all manner of experiments, and whether he succeeds or fails, he secures his object – agreeable occupation. The professional has all his energies directed to make things pay. He has too much at stake to speculate.[8]

Lady Hawarden's photography was a great deal more than an agreeable occupation. Her large output, constant variations on set themes and sheer originality suggest a driven, even obsessive, activity. However, her work remained unpublished at the time of her death from pneumonia in 1865, aged 42. None was acquired by the Museum in her short lifetime. Her oeuvre was given by her granddaughter in 1939, as will be related in the next chapter.

Lady Hawarden's use of mirrors and windows contrasts with the polished games of Camille Silvy. There were many ways to adjust the lighting in his sophisticated studio, which was just the other side of Hyde Park from Lady Hawarden's. In her photographs the lighting behaves more naturally and therefore more unpredictably. She used light to dissolve form as well as to define it. While Silvy's compositions are adroitly posed, in mocked-up studies, libraries or landscapes, and carefully furnished with accessories, Hawarden's are less easily legible, arranged in real but generally empty rooms, and replete with ambiguity. Here, in Plate 35, there is an implication that the window has become a mirror in which each sister sees her *alter ego*. Silvy's elegantly photographed women are dressed in the height of fashion, whereas Hawarden often photographed her daughters *en déshabillé*, but also with the sharp, natural lighting of modernity.

The creative instability of the image in Lady Hawarden's photographs was – and is – matched by the general uncertainties mentioned at the beginning of this chapter. How should the medium of photography be classified? The most striking test case occurred in 1861. The Commissioners of the International Exhibition to be held in

South Kensington the following year decided not to classify photography with fine art but, to the consternation of photographers in both London and Paris, with machinery. As Steve Edwards has pointed out in a subtle essay, the Commissioners' classification reflected the taxonomic principles on which the whole vast exhibition was organized, a taxonomy based upon a particular view of the value of labour.[9]

The Commissioners were besieged by photographers and supporters of the stature of Frederick Pollock, the Lord Chief Baron, arguing against the demeaning classification. Finally a compromise was found. Photography was provided for as a class on its own, neither fine art nor machinery but 'an independent art'. This may sound Olympian – and is, in fact, the perfect formulation – but the reality was a taxonomic fudge and the practical result an unworkable space. British photographers found their prints hung in a room in the glass dome of the exhibition building, reached by awkward backstairs, crowded with photographic equipment and shared with educational aids. Many photographs faded rapidly because of the combination of newly painted walls and intense heat, which also exploded bottles of collodion.[10]

This débâcle may have been one of the reasons for Roger Fenton's departure from photography in 1862. However, for all its faults, the occasion had provided an opportunity for important acquisitions. And a handful were made. Photographs appeared at many points in the exhibition, sometimes as works of art in their own right, sometimes illustrating manufacturing processes or 'art designs'. In total, there were about 2,000 frames (some containing many photographs), from over 400 contributors, at 25 different places in the show. A handsome series of large-scale photographs of leather-working crafts had been commissioned by the firm of Bevingtons in Bermondsey, East London. The photographs were skilfully undertaken by Geoffrey Bevington, a younger member of the family firm.[11] The set was acquired for the Photography Collection, as was a series of portraits on leather from Prince Edward Island, Canada.

An English sculptor, Joseph Barlow Robinson of Derby, was fascinated by the British photographic display. He wrote to many of the exhibitors asking for specimens of their work. The large album that he assembled contains correspondence and original photographs by English exhibitors, plus engravings of cameras and other equipment. There is a note from Talbot, as well as specimens of the process by which he had linked photography to ink printing. He named these photoglyphic prints and by 1880 they had stimulated the invention, by Karel Klic, of photogravure. (Examples of the technique are illustrated later in this chapter.) As in 1858, the Museum did not collect systematically from the 1862 International Exhibition but benefited from the prescience of a private enthusiast. Robinson's unique album was given to the Museum in 1961 by Miss Sarah E. Eaton, in memory of Miss Isabella Kerr Robinson.

Photography's identity problems did not daunt the robust and spirited Julia Margaret Cameron. Another hybrid, she was of Anglo-Indian background – or rather, as her mother was French, Franglo-Indian. Cameron acquired her first camera late in 1863 at the age of 48. Faced with the bourgeois Lilliputians of the cartes craze, Cameron opted for the heroic – for heads, sometimes, of life-size. Her experiments were radical and her methods bold. If parts of a negative dissatisfied her she scraped away the collodion, and printed what remained. She made montages, printing from two negatives on one sheet: the abruptness of these procedures has become attractive to modern eyes. She might scratch architectural details, or a halo, on her negatives. She printed 'day-for-night', as Bill Brandt did in the 1930s, and (like Brandt) added a moon if the subject required one. She adopted a practice as opposed as possible to the new commercial norm.

Among the literary and other lions she invited to sit for her was Henry Cole. The sitting took place at the Kensington house of Cameron's sister Sara and her painter husband Val Prinsep. Cole recorded in his diary for Friday, 19 May 1865: 'To Mrs Cameron Little Holland House to have my portrait taken in her style. A German girl held an umbrella over me. Mr Prinsep assisting, & the Irish Girls. Saw Watts...'[12] Both Val Prinsep and G.F. Watts had been commissioned to design parts of an ambitious cycle of murals at the South Kensington Museum and there were other mutual friends, such as Annie and Minnie Thackeray. Besides, Cameron's brief but daring career in photography had already inspired considerable comment. Her portraits, often deliberately out-of-focus, were well known. Five letters from Cameron to Cole are preserved among the correspondence in the National Art Library. Although she was a prolific correspondent, few of Cameron's letters on photographic matters appear to have survived. These previously unpublished examples give a fresh insight into the photographer, her work and her relations with the South Kensington Museum.[13]

She had the energy of a force of nature and a faith in her work to move mountains. She wrote to Cole on 20 May 1865, from Little Holland House, at top speed and omitting full stops: 'I have real pleasure in telling you that Mr Watts thinks my photograph of you "extremely fine" I hope to tone & wash tonight after a day's *most* arduous work I really fear even my energies breaking down with the work of today. All yesty. I took studies of Lady Elcho & Lord Elcho said they were the finest things *ever* done in Art! The day before I took 12 portraits and the same day or rather night I toned & printed & I washed six dozen – therefore I write this word standing midst work'. She arranged for her dealer, Colnaghi, to send Cole a complete portfolio of her work: 'I should be so proud and pleased if this complete series could go into the South Kensington Museum... I leave on Monday by the 11 am train today I have Lord Elcho and Lord Overstone Browning & several ladies all coming to sit & my strength is well nigh spent'. She gave the Museum the Browning portrait that autumn.

The portrait of Cole turned out well and a print is in the collection of the Royal

Society of Arts. He arranged for the Museum to buy a collection of Cameron's photographs – her first sale to a Museum. She had been photographing for about eighteen months. Cole bought 80 prints. There was a set for the Art Library and further sets for the Circulation Department. The Museum's payment of £22.4s.4d. on 10 August 1865 must have marked one of the better days of Cameron's career. On 27 September 1865 Cameron, with characteristic open-handedness, sent 34 mounted photographs: 'These photographs are presented to the Museum by Mrs Cameron as specimens of her photography'.

Why did Cole buy these photographs? After all, the Museum had acquired nothing from Lady Hawarden, who lived and worked in the heart of his South Kensington milieu. There is a clue in the Photography Collection Registers, the volumes in which each new acquisition was recorded and numbered as it arrived in the Art Library. Four of the Cameron photographs were 'presented' by Cole to the Museum's chief designer Godfrey Sykes. At that time Sykes was designing columns for a new entrance to the expanding museum, ornamented with many figures, mainly of women and children, in terracotta. They are still to be seen in the Pirelli Garden. Sykes designed them and their decorative figures in a Quattrocento style. Many of the Cameron photographs acquired in 1865 are in a similar style, reminiscent of the sculptures of Desiderio da Settignano and other masters. The Sykes figures may owe no debts at all to Cameron's madonnas, saints and children, but it seems very likely that Cole acquired the photographs, at least in part, because he saw them as potentially inspiring for designers. Maybe that is how Cameron presented her work to Cole. She printed a revealing sentence in the catalogue of her exhibition at the French Gallery that autumn. From one point of view it reveals extraordinary *chutzpah*, but it was no doubt sincerely and modestly meant: 'All artists are allowed to purchase at half price'.

South Kensington was the first museum to exhibit Cameron's photographs, when Cole displayed a selection of them in Autumn 1865. It is not known which or how many. 'They are very beautiful', wrote Cameron's friend Kate Perry, 'and as usual she treats the many-headed monster, the public, as her dear familiar, writing in large hand on these photographs, MY GRANDCHILD, JULIA MARGARET NORMAN, aged 6, with her nurse, and so on'.[14] In the *British Journal of Photography* for 3 November, the critic A.H. Wall wrote of Cameron's photographs being 'awarded a prominent place at the South Kensington Museum close to the picture collections, where they hang "in their pride alone".' By that, Wall meant that Cameron's were the only photographs 'from life', the phrase she carefully inscribed on her mounts. Photographs of works of art, architecture and design were, like plaster casts and electrotypes, plentifully used in the Museum's displays.

Wall was, it seems, the only reviewer to notice the Camerons among the vast and varied exhibition. Raphael's cartoons for tapestries had just arrived from Hampton

Court, on loan from Queen Victoria, and been regally installed. The new displays also included, as a writer in *The Illustrated London News* noted, 'mosaic work, enamels, ceramics, church and other furniture, jewellery, engraved gems, arms and ornamental work in the base and precious metals, and casts of the same, watches, coffers, Venetian and other glass, vestments, dresses, draperies of many kinds, Indian embroidered fabrics, lace of various countries and dates, specimens of stained glass, miniatures and snuff-boxes' (and two more paragraphs in the same vein).[15]

However, Wall not only picked out Cameron's photographs, but wrote of them well. As in Old Master paintings, he observed, 'one uniform tone unites the whole into a kind of conventional unity, so in these photographs a pale grey veils alike the deepest shadows and the highest lights...' Mrs Cameron achieved this effect by making long exposures in low light. That is why the German girl held an umbrella over Henry Cole. Indeed, an umbrella handle is visible in the portrait of William Michael Rossetti dressed as a Renaissance grandee – one of the photographs acquired in 1865. The tone was not always grey, of course. It could be a rich purple from the gold toning bath, depending on the printing batch. The croppings vary too. Sometimes the tiny white spots which blemish prints have been retouched, sometimes not. In fact, astonishingly, there are no true duplicates among all the prints acquired in 1865.

Whatever Cole's exact motivation for acquiring Mrs Cameron's work, he brought into the collection some of the most extraordinary photographic images ever conceived and made. Two prints of *Floss and Iolande* were among them (Plate 36). Here the forms have dissolved into each other even more completely than in Lady Hawarden's work. This is almost a 'spirit photograph'. Swirls of collodion film on the negative merge ambiguously with swirling draperies. Floss and Iolande are characters in *St Clement's Eve*, a play by Cameron's intimate friend Sir Henry Taylor.

The interpretation of Cameron's iconography has been transformed in recent years by Dr Mike Weaver, Reader in American Literature at the University of Oxford, who describes himself as an 'amateur' of photographic history. Weaver produced the touring exhibition *Julia Margaret Cameron, 1815–1879* in 1984, which received its final showing at the V&A in 1985. Exactly 120 years after her work was first shown in South Kensington, Cameron's photographs were shown again, alongside paintings by Watts, prints of the period and publications by the Arundel Society (of which she was a member). Weaver's catalogue rediscovered Cameron's intellectual milieu. 'Hitherto,' he argued, 'Cameron's photographs have been seen as vaguely allegorical, but they are more properly described as typological or typical – illustrative in a profound, biblical sense':

> A biblical type may be said to represent a person or event in the Bible, who or which can be seen to correspond to other such types, or anti-types. For

36. Julia Margaret Cameron (British, 1815–79). **Floss and Iolande**, 1864. Albumen print. Title inscribed on the mount in pencil. 9⅝ × 7⅝ in (24.5 × 19.5 cm). Bought from the photographer, 1865. 44.755.

instance, King David is an anti-type of Christ. The comparison of such types involves not only biblical criticism or interpretation, but a Christian psychology. Infinite aspects of Christian behaviour can be observed by endless comparisons between such types. It is a serial process in which one type illustrates another with overtones of meaning accruing to the types as one is metamorphosed into another.[16]

37. JULIA MARGARET CAMERON (British, 1815–79). **Alfred, Lord Tennyson**, 3 June 1869. Albumen print. 12 × 9⁹⁄₁₆ in (30.4 × 24.4 cm). Given by Alan S. Cole. 932–1913.

Weaver had found a key to understanding Cameron's imagery in the writings of her contemporary Anna Jameson, especially the work first published as *The Poetry of Sacred and Legendary Art* in 1848. *Floss and Iolande* has much in common with the Visitation (of Elizabeth to the Virgin Mary in Luke 1, 39–56).[17] The theme of the female embrace appears elsewhere in Cameron's work, notably in *The Kiss of Peace* (1869).[18]

Cameron wrote again to Cole on 22 February 1866:

I write to ask if you will be having any photographic soiree or meeting soon at which I may send to the Science & Art Dept. for you to exhibit at the South Kensington Museum a set of prints of my late series of photographs that I intend should *electrify* you with delight & startle the world. I hope it is no vain imagination of mine to say the like have never been produced and never can be surpassed! ... Seeing is believing & you shall see & the world shall see if you can create for me a great occasion! because these wonderful photographs should come out all at *once* & take the world by surprise! ... Mr Thurston Thompson I hope *will* be delighted this time.

Won't the South Kensington Museum give me a crown! Not of diamond stones but those diamonds laurels – or a medal or honorable [*sic*] mention if this series of photographs of mine surpasses all others –

Talk of roundness I have it in perfect perfection...

A postscript adds that Cameron had set aside a parcel of prints of earlier works for Mrs Cole. It is interesting that Cole had bought Cameron's work for the Museum despite Thurston Thompson's apparent lack of enthusiasm for it. Cole did not, it seems, hold a soirée, organize an exhibition or otherwise promote Cameron's new work: perhaps he felt that, as a civil servant, he could go no further at that time. However, he would go further, as we shall see.

She wrote next on 7 April 1868 on technical matters. She disliked the prints that Cole had shown her by 'Mr Pouncey' – presumably John Pouncey, who devised various techniques for printing photographs permanently in inks and pigments. Beginning with commments on Pouncey's technique, Cameron goes on to tell us what she strived for in her own:

It is beautifully and carefully done but I cannot say that I think the artistic character of photography is preserved. I should like to hear the opinion of Mr

> Watts & other artists on this subject. I think as you say that for House Decoration & for things seen from afar this process ought to have a brilliant success but for any thing so delicate as a portrait the shining glazed surface destroys the pleasure by giving a sticking plaster look & I think that even in oil painting any thick layer of varnish is a great injury to the effect. It is the dull quiet surface of a photograph however rich in tone & tint it may be that constitutes I think the harmony of the work...

38. Julia Margaret Cameron (British, 1815–79). **The Dream**, 1869. Albumen print. Inscribed on the mount: '"Quite Divine" – G.F. Watts. From life registered Freshwater April 1869'. Copyright Julia Margaret Cameron. 11 15/16 × 9 9/16 in (30.3 × 24.2 cm). Given by Alan S. Cole, 1913. 947–1913.

The letter goes on to thank Cole for lending her rooms at the Museum for portrait sessions and to let him know of forthcoming sittings with Lord Granville (Cole's superior), Mr Whitworth, HRH (His or Her Royal Highness, but which?) '& other Royal sitters you may obtain for me. I will come up & work with renewed energy at your Museum after the fortnight of refreshing change I shall have here.' She had photographed Cole's daughter Isabella, and was highly gratified that Mr Spartali had ordered 40 copies of her portrait of his daughter Marie, and sent her 20 guineas. Mr Dan Gurney had sent an order for 24 prints and a cheque for £12.10s.:

> Lord Essex will do the same & all this I tell you to shew you that [through] this your gracious loan of those two rooms I am likely now to acquire fortune as well as fame for as I told you & you gave me entire sympathy a woman with sons to educate cannot live on fame alone! I owe the start to you & I hope I shall win a good race & win a diadem as well as a gold crown!

Cameron was not averse to taking commercial portraits, as she – in her brief *Annals of My Glass House* (1874) – and later commentators have liked to suggest. The collection includes a portrait of Louise-Béatrice de Fonblanque inscribed by Cameron 'Taken at the South Kensington Museum'. Cole seems to have gone a very long way in supporting her by lending rooms in the Museum and, possibly, helping to find sitters. No wonder, then, that when Cameron wrote again on 12 June 1869, she opened with thanks and a gift:

> I have so perpetually remembered all yr. helping kindness & ever friendly hand [?] to me in the earlier years of my Art that I delight in now sending you four of my latest works as my grateful gift to you including the very latest of all, my last portrait of Alfred Tennyson (not yet published) which I think you will agree with me in feeling is a National Treasure of immense value – next to the living speaking man must ever stand this portrait of him, quite the most faithful & most noble Portrait of him existing [Plate 37] – surely this Portrait ought to be engraved for altho' I can ensure thro' my own care the durability of my *print*, I can alas do nothing to make durable the far more precious original negative. The chemicals supplied to me for this are beyond my power & prove fatally perishable. 45 of my most precious negatives this year have perished thro the

fault of collodion or glass supplied: both or either destroy the film that holds the picture – you will see in the Dream [Plate 38] the commencement of this cruel calamity [the lines on the head-dress] – also in the Guardian Angel – which has overtaken 45 of my *Gems* – a honeycomb crack extending over the picture appearing at any moment and beyond my power to arrest.

39. EADWEARD MUYBRIDGE (American, born England, 1830–1904). Dancing couple from **Animal Locomotion**, 1887. Collotype. 11 × 10¼ in (28.2 × 26.5 cm). Bought by subscription, 1887. 711–1889.

She had taken her problem to a meeting of the Photographic Society and, she wrote, received 50–60 different answers from the 50–60 professional photographers present: 'All were in error as no reason explained why all the negatives of my first four years are as perfect as the day on which they were done – a change in the manufacture of varnish & collodion only explains the change to me'. She resolved 'to print as actively as I can whilst my precious negative is yet good Secondly to try to get Portraits I have taken of our greatest men engraved.' In the event, she had her portraits printed in the permanent carbon process by the Autotype Company. 'Think with a generous head,' she implored Cole 'what you can do for me – & will you? Are there no Schools of Art for which you can send me orders – Is there no corner of the S.K. Museum where you can install me? You know I have my Gold Medal – but even now after five years of toil I have not yet by One Hundred Pounds recovered the money I have spent'. Her final letter to Cole, on 24 December 1872, asked his advice about practical arrangements at the Universal Exhibition in Vienna (1873).

Apart from showing Mrs Cameron in South Kensington, the Museum circulated her work nationwide, and probably for several years, through its Circulation Department. This was the largest operation of its kind in the world. In a speech given in 1873, on the eve of his retirement, Cole spoke of the astonishing scale of the Museum's outreach: 'Whilst this Museum itself has been visited by more than twelve millions of visitors, it has circulated objects to one hundred and ninety-five localities holding exhibitions, to which more than four millions of local visitors have contributed above ninety-three thousand pounds.'[19]

In 1870 the Museum had exhibited *Engravings, Prints, and Photographs* from the collection of S.T. Davenport, an official at the Society of Arts. This survey included many of the key photographic processes of photography's first thirty years, a significant number of which were British inventions. The exhibition showed Talbot's calotypes and photoglyphs, photo-galvanographs (rather fuzzy ink-prints which the Museum itself had bought in their 1850s heyday), carbon prints, Woodburytypes, Albertypes, photolithographs and finally 'Composition Photographs', including Rejlander's *Two Ways of Life* and works by Robinson and Cherrill. The collection was not acquired, nor was there a desire on the part of the Museum to collect photographic processes and techniques systematically.

Very shortly after this survey was shown, another major breakthrough was made for photography by a British scientist. The gelatin dry plate process was proposed by

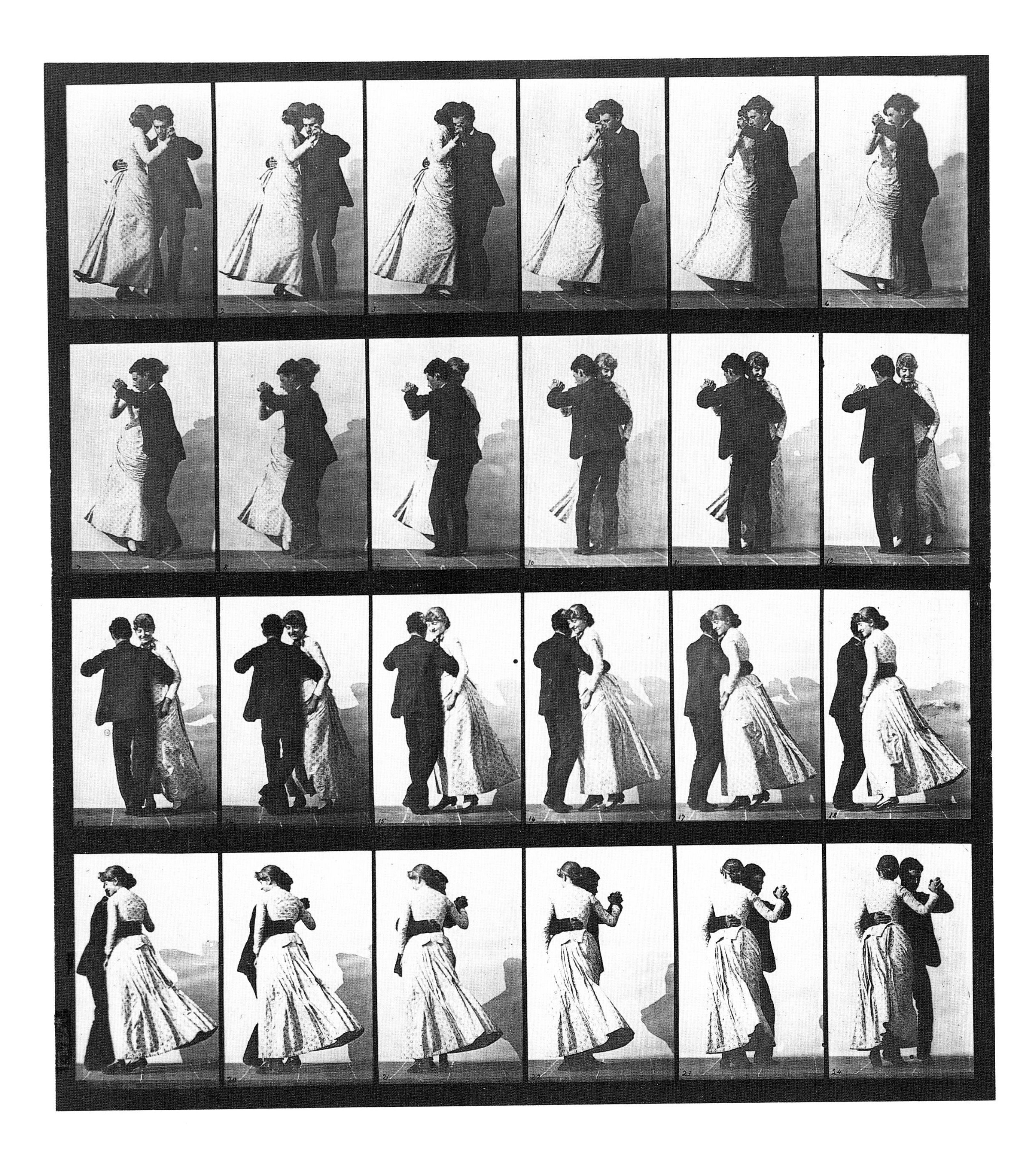

40. PAUL MARTIN (British, born Alsace, 1864–1944). **The Crowd Waiting to See a Policeman's Funeral**, 1894. Platinum print. 3 × 4 in (7.7 × 10 cm). Bought 1980. 1799–1980.

(opposite)
41. PETER HENRY EMERSON (American, worked Britain, 1856–1936). **Breezy Marshland**, 1889. Photogravure. 14½ × 21⅝ in (37 × 55 cm). Transferred from the Prints Collection, 1896. 2126–1896.

Dr R.L. Maddox in 1871. After various improvements it went into production in 1878 and rapidly replaced the wet collodion process. The new plates were evenly coated by machine, were bought ready-to-use, and were vastly more sensitive than anything available before. The process remained in use for the next hundred years. Another key invention was platinum printing paper, introduced by William Willis in 1879. Its delicate tonal gradations and matt surface were often compared to mezzotint.

There was soon to be a remarkable demonstration of the possibilities of the astonishing speed of the gelatin dry plate. This was the ambitious portfolio *Animal Locomotion: An Electrophotographic Investigation of Consecutive Phases of Animal Movement* (Plate 39). The South Kensington Museum was one of the subscribers to this landmark publication by the English emigrant to the United States, Eadweard Muybridge. (Subscribers guaranteed an initial number of sales of an expensive work, thus ensuring that a publication was viable before production began.) The University of Pennsylvania brought out the work in 1887. Again, as with the work of Henry Taylor in the 1850s and Julia Margaret Cameron in the 1860s, there is a link between these instantaneous photographs, with their dramatic modernity, and the education of artists. The most illustrious painter known to have used the Muybridge plates is Francis Bacon. The art critic David Sylvester vividly remembers Bacon talking of his visits to the V&A to see the plates in the Winter of 1949–50.

The technical transformation of photography in the last quarter of the nineteenth century embraced not only fast exposure times but also the beginnings of the half-tone revolution. Before the 1890s photographs used in magazines always needed to be translated into engravings. In 1852 Talbot had suggested the idea of breaking up a photographic image into small dots to facilitate making a printing plate; but the technique did not receive commercial application until the early 1880s.

P.H.EMERSON.

Paul Martin is one of the figures who epitomizes the change from the technology of wood engraving and line block to photography and half-tone. Born in France in 1864, Martin and his family came to Britain as refugees from the Franco-Prussian War of 1870. He was apprenticed as a wood-engraver and trained in the London firm of Paul Douet from 1880 to 1886, when the half-tone process was already beginning to emerge as the new method of illustration. In London, wood-engraving firms fell away, just as the portrait-miniature studios had before them. Between 1884 and 1889 the number of wood-engraving businesses dropped from 162 to 80. Process-engraving firms grew from 6 to 56. The number of professional photographers jumped from 6,661 in 1881 to 10,571 in 1891 and 14,999 in 1901. Looking back in 1939 Paul Martin recalled: 'Few wood-engravers realized what photography was going to bring in its train. I knew that monster when he was only a sprat, for I took up photography as an amateur in 1884... When the monster made a lunge at me I dodged him and clung to his tail and am still hanging on'.[20]

Paul Martin became one of the most adept users of the 'Detective' cameras in vogue in the last two decades of the nineteenth century. The camera was disguised, typically, as a leather-covered box. This was the beginning of the so-called 'Candid Camera'. However, the camera was not always concealed. Martin's photograph of *The Crowd Waiting to See a Policeman's Funeral* (1894) (Plate 40) is an early example of the camera's effect on behaviour. The policeman did not react favourably, but a girl behind him was thrilled. Such photographs anticipate kindred images by later photojournalists. However, it was not until the 1930s, the heyday of photographically illustrated magazines, that the Museum acquired any of Martin's work, as will be seen in the next chapter.

Apart from Muybridge, during the 1880s and 1890s the Museum was acquiring the work of another Anglo-American photographer in depth. Peter Henry Emerson (1856–1936) was born in Cuba, then a Spanish colony. His father was American and his mother English. Brought up in Cuba, the United States and – from the age of 14 – England, he trained as a doctor but never practised. Instead he began to photograph and write. In 1882 Emerson joined the Photographic Society and published a novel. He made use of the new possibilities of the 1880s – the gelatin dry-plate negative, full-toned, matt platinum paper and high-quality ink printing in photogravure. He also made use of his talent for writing, and his knowledge of contemporary painters and painting.

Inspired by such artists as Bastien-Lepage, Clausen, his friend Thomas Goodall, Lhermitte, La Thangue and Whistler, Emerson championed pictorial photography, a key phrase of the time, against mere topography. True landscape photography, he argued in lectures, articles and the book *Naturalistic Photography for Students of the Art* (1889), conveyed the feel and look of the whole instead of an accumulation of separate facts. He emphasized aerial perspective, soft contours and differential

42. Peter Henry Emerson (American, worked Britain, 1856–1936). **Flowers o' the Mere**, 1887. Photogravure. 2¾ × 2¾ in (7.2 × 7.2 cm). E.1081–1996.

focusing, which allowed for relatively sharper focus on a chief point of interest set off against more vaguely registered surroundings. These qualities are exemplified by his large-scale photogravure *Breezy Marshland* (1889) (Plate 41). He also worked on a small scale and printed in orange ink, bringing photography into an intimate relationship with printmaking (Plate 42). In the manner of a traditional graphic artist, Emerson destroyed negatives and cancelled photogravure plates once editions had been printed.

He also cancelled his views on photography, publishing *The Death of Naturalistic Photography* in 1890. He followed this up with 'A Renunciation to all Photographers' addressed to readers of the *British Journal of Photography* (23 January 1891):

> The limitations of photography are so great that, though the results may and sometimes do give a certain aesthetic pleasure, the medium must always rank the lowest of all arts, lower than any graphic art, for the individuality of the artist is cramped; in short, it can scarcely show itself... Photography is first of all the hand-maiden of art and science.[21]

Although the authorities at South Kensington would have agreed, talented photographers of the time did not. The Linked Ring Brotherhood, formed in 1892, described itself as 'a means of bringing together those who are interested in the development of the highest form of Art of which Photography is capable'. It aimed to be 'a sociable coterie of picture-loving, as separate from purely scientific or practical craftsmen'.[22] The core of the group seceded from the Photographic Society of Great Britain (which was to be granted a royal charter two years later). The long-deepening schism between photographic artists and science/commerce opened into clear splits in different centres almost simultaneously.[23] The idea of secesssion from technical and commercial photography occurred in quick succession in Vienna, London, Hamburg and Paris between 1891 and 1894. New York's Photo-Secession, organized by Alfred Stieglitz, followed in 1902. The Linked Ring drew on such models as the Century Guild, an association of craft workers (1882–c.1889), and the New English Art Club, formed in 1886 by painters who had broken away from the Royal Academy.

Frederick H. Hollyer was among the earliest of the 'Links', elected in June 1892. Like Paul Martin, Hollyer had started out in one of the traditional print media. He began his career, Anne Kelsey Hammond writes, 'as a reproductive engraver of paintings in mezzotint – the process of engraving which bears the greatest likeness, in its velvety surface and its subtle range of tones, to the platinotype'.[24] Hollyer joined the Photographic Society in 1865, photographed William Morris, Edward Burne-Jones and their families in 1874, and became an outstanding interpreter of works of art. He was awarded the major medal in this class at the Paris Exhibition in 1889. The South Kensington Museum acquired many of Hollyer's exquisite platinotypes after works by Burne-Jones, Rossetti and others at that time. An exhibition of his copies of the work of Burne-Jones was held in the Museum in 1899.[25]

There were other sides to Hollyer which the Museum ignored, however: his landscapes, interiors, still-lifes and portraits. The Museum did accumulate a large corpus impressively titled 'The British Museum of Portraits, South Kensington Collection', taken and donated by A.J. Melhuish between 1864 and 1896. The low value of these mediocre portraits is further reduced by heavy retouching. Hollyer's portraits, on the contrary, were imbued with the Morrisian virtue of truth to materials. He sounds both Morrisian and modern when he argues in 1896, in the pages of *The Studio* – a lively new magazine of fine and applied arts – that: 'In other arts, especially the subsidiary, it is their very limitations which the craftsmen turn with instinctive recognition to their own advantage. If this principle were only to be recognised and honestly lived up to by photographers in general, we should have results which would be better art, because they would be better photographs'.[26]

Hollyer is the finest chronicler of the personalities of the Arts and Crafts Movement, together with the overlapping worlds of writers, social thinkers, scientists, actors and actresses, painters and other talented photographers of the time. His portraits are preserved in three chintz-covered albums assembled for his daughter Eleanor in 1920; she in turn presented them to the Museum in 1938. He is the judicious platinotype-period counterpart of Mrs Cameron. Like her, he was capable of considerable variation in method. For Margaret Burne-Jones, whom he had known since she was a child, he contrived the simplest silhouette and most delicate separation of tonal values (Plate 43). He chose a more animated, sociable setting for Mrs Patrick Campbell, the finest actress of his day and a notable wit. He photographed her in 1893 when she rose to fame in the title role of Sir Arthur Pinero's *The Second Mrs Tanqueray* (Plate 44). She published two of Hollyer's portraits in *My Life and Some Letters* (1922).

43. FREDERICK HOLLYER (British, 1837–1933). **Margaret Burne-Jones**, *c.*1890. Platinum print. 5¾ × 4 in (14.7 × 10 cm). Given by Eleanor M. Hollyer, 1938. 7818–1938.

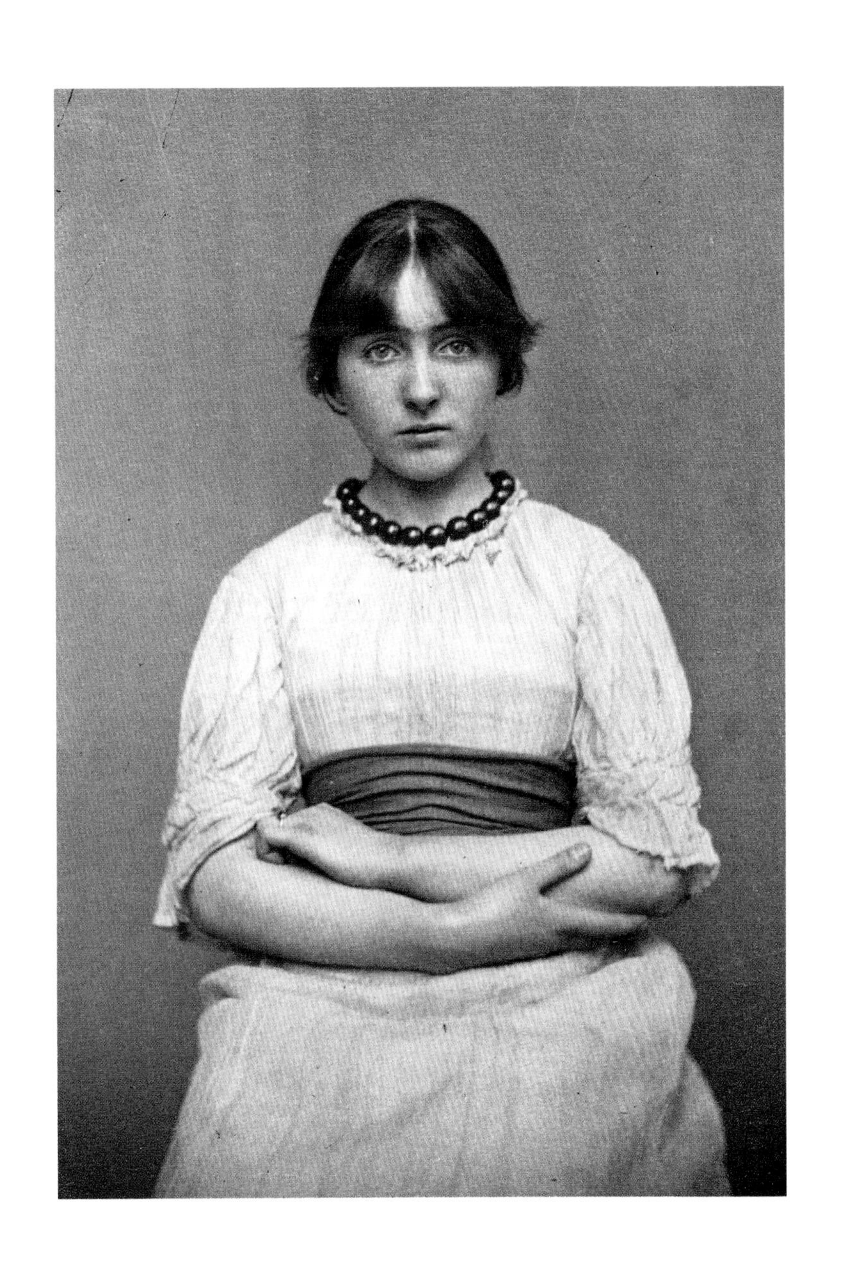

44. FREDERICK HOLLYER (British, 1837–1933). **Mrs Patrick Campbell**, 1893. Platinum print. 4 × 5¾ in (10 × 14.7 cm). Given by Eleanor M. Hollyer, 1938. 7860–1938.

Although theatrical greatness is ephemeral, Mrs Pat, as she was affectionately known, remains immortal. This is partly because of such observations as 'Marriage is the result of the longing for the deep, deep peace of the double bed after the hurly burly of the chaise-longue' and 'I don't mind where people make love, so long as they don't do it in the street and frighten the horses'. Not to spoil a favourite quotation, but the phrase 'make love' has changed its meaning quite as much as the word 'art' over the same period. The first changed from something like 'to display amorous interest'. 'Art' moved along a scale from 'craft' or 'skill' to 'fine art'. Raymond Williams charted the shift in *Keywords* (1983).

Another word with a shifting value was 'amateur'. It began to slide from its original meaning – one who practises a given activity purely for the love of it – to the less flattering implications enshrined in 'amateurish' and 'rank amateur'. Hollyer used it in the earlier sense when he remarked that 'it would be a most useful thing, even from a business point of view, if every photographer would resolve that for every negative made for profit there should be another made for love'. Hollyer summed up one of the themes of this chapter when he added that 'the best professional photographers could do some of the finest amateur work'.[27]

Frederick H. Evans, also a member of the Linked Ring, worked in the same spirit. His photographs of English cathedral architecture were informed by his ardent admiration of William Morris. They also look forward to the geometry of the twentieth century. This is especially true of *Lincoln Cathedral: Stairway in Southwest Turret* (Plate 45). The image also looks forward in another way. Although Evans was, like Hollyer, a master of the platinum process, this is an ink print, a photogravure. It was produced for Evans in 1900, two years after he made the original negative. Evans held an important solo exhibition of some 150 works in 1900. In his opening address he referred to the photogravures made for him by the Swan Electric Engraving Co. of 'four of my finest things'.[28] He gave the four prints to the Museum the same year. For much of the new century photography would be transmitted not in the form of silver or platinum-based prints but in ink.

Actually, Evans did not give the four photogravures to the South Kensington Museum, strictly speaking. That institution was also being transformed by the splits and schisms characteristic of the end of the century. The ever-broadening, constantly deepening, collections in South Kensington were proving too various as well as too vast. In the years since Cole's retirement in 1874, the Museum had, critics said, begun to lose its way. A government inquiry into the Museums of the Department of Science and Art began in 1896. The inquiry was exhaustive. It must have been terrifying for W.H.J. Weale, the Librarian. Members of Parliament asked him to explain the bizarre numbering sequence of the Photography Collection. An index to the collection published in 1868 purported to begin at number one but actually began with number 31,623. Mr Weale did not know why, although another witness explained that the earlier numbers had been allotted to prints. The numbering system had been changed in 1885 to a more convenient system in which each photograph was allotted a number followed by a dash and the year of acquisition (for example, 1–1885). The same principle applies today, prefixed by E. The evidence to the select committee revealed a breakdown of trust between Director and Librarian and the fact that 'an attendant' was in day-to-day charge of the Photography Collection. A new man, T.C. Grove, took charge of the Photography Collection as Assistant Keeper in 1896. We shall learn more of his view of the collection in the following chapter.

The select committee did not inquire into photography as any form of art in its own right, but was concerned exclusively with its role in copying and diffusing works of art. The Museum was proud of the service it provided in this area. At the catalogue stall, visitors could look through an inventory of photographs of works of art and architecture taken by Fratelli Alinari in Florence. Alinari photographs could be ordered in the shop and, at a cost of 6½d., were despatched direct to the visitor: sixpence paid for the print and a halfpenny for the postage. This was, indeed, a remarkable service. Photography was still seen as a wonderfully efficient, low-cost method of distributing information about art.

The select committee's report made large recommendations. A new building should be constructed to house the collections securely. The Science Museum was to become a separate administrative entity on the west side of Exhibition Road. The Art Museum was to be divided into material-based curatorial departments: Architecture and Sculpture, Ceramics and so on.[29] In 1899 Queen Victoria, on the final public appearance of her long reign, laid the foundation stone of a new building designed by Sir Aston Webb on Cromwell Road. She renamed the institution the Victoria and Albert Museum. The occasion was recorded in a sequence of instantaneous photographs. Flickering images show the old lady, her entourage and shining coach, a student presenting a bouquet among the nodding ostrich plumes, the milling crowd. The sequence was viewed by peering through the eyepiece of an American-designed 'Mutoscope' and turning a handle: a portent of things to come.

45. Frederick H. Evans (British, 1853–1943). **Lincoln Cathedral: Stairway in Southwest Turret**, 1898. Photogravure (printed 1900). 7⅞ × 5⅜ in (20 × 13.7 cm). Given by the photographer, 1900. 595–1900.

CHAPTER FIVE

The Cosmopolitan Archive

From the beginning the South Kensington Museum had included Science Collections, often called the Science Museum, housed in galleries on the west side of Exhibition Road. From 1908 the Science Museum became a separate institution with its own administration – and its own Photography Collection. Pressure for a separate Science Museum dated back to an exhibition titled *The Loan Collection of Scientific Instruments and Apparatus* (1876). The display, with a catalogue already in its third edition by 1877, included an impressive photography section. This embraced a haphazard but still remarkable range of photographic processes, plus apparatus. A highlight was the lens 'with which the pictures of Mr Fox Talbot's Pencil of Nature were taken' (cat. no. 954b). This and other important items were acquired for the Scientific Collections. Later acquisitions included the donation in 1890 of 158 Daguerreotypes taken in Italy by A.J. Ellis. This was the nucleus for the expansion that occurred – dramatically, as we shall see – in the newly independent Science Museum in the next decades.

Another initiative was the creation of a Department of Engraving, Illustration and Design at the V&A in 1909. This drew its collection from the loose sheets and bound volumes of prints and drawings that had been accumulated by the Art Library since 1852 (and even earlier, going back to the first School of Design). The new department had been a subdivision of the Art Library, like the photographs section. However, the field of prints and drawings was a mature collecting area. The Museum had already published, in 1905, a catalogue by Martin Hardie of its Whistler prints, for example. Whistler understandably cast a long shadow on photography.

This can be seen in the early career of Edward Steichen, who founded the American Photo-Secession with Alfred Stieglitz in New York in 1902. Five years later Stieglitz, the leader of American art photography, was photographed by Heinrich Kühn, the leader of European art photography. The Steichen gum platinum portrait of Anatole France (Plate 46), made in Paris in 1909, and the Kühn oil pigment portrait of Stieglitz, made in Innsbruck in 1907 (Plate 47), are highly manipulated fine photographs of the Photo-Secession period. Anatole France shoots immaculately starched cuffs. A sculptured torso can be discerned in the bright dusk of the famous writer's inner sanctum. Such veiled nuances were the essence of Photo-Secession style. In Kühn's Innsbruck studio, panelled in the same Arts and Crafts style as Frederick Hollyer's portrait rooms in Kensington, Alfred Stieglitz rises – majestically cloaked – above formlessness and darkness.

46. Edward Steichen (American, 1879–1973). **Portrait of Anatole France**, 1909. Gum platinum print. 12⅞ × 9⅞ in (32.7 × 25 cm). Bought 1976. 39–1977.

Although the Museum bought a tenebrous lithographed head by Eugène Carrière in 1903, no grand photographic *tours de force* were acquired during the heyday of the Photo-Secession. These portraits were bought only 70 years later – in 1976, the year before the Photography Collection in turn left the Art Library (as we shall see in chapter seven). The understanding of photography was very different from the print connoisseurship that was acknowledged by the creation of the Department of Engravings, Illustration and Design in 1909.

47. HEINRICH KÜHN (German, worked Austria, 1866–1944). **Portrait of Alfred Stieglitz**, 1907. Oil pigment print. 11⅜ × 8⅞ in (28.9 × 22.7 cm). Bought 1976. 38–1977.

T.C. Grove wrote a 'Report on Photograph Section' dated 12 June 1908. As a result of the select committee's recommendations, mentioned in the previous chapter, Grove had been appointed Assistant Keeper in charge of photographs in 1897. The committee had not been impressed by past cataloguing. The Library's Keeper had reported that the collection might number about 100,000 photographs. In 1908, Grove estimated that the total could be as high as 200,000. It was hard for him to be sure, as there were many duplicates, triplicates, etc., and he believed that earlier practice had been simply to give one number to each subject, regardless of how many further copies there were. Sometimes albums containing many photographs were allotted just one number.

Since 1897 a new system for classifying the photographs had been introduced. There were 35 headings. One of these was 'Studies for Painting' (Class XXIVC). This classification is inscribed, for example, on the mount of Henry Taylor's *Bryony* (Figure 4) and some of Mrs Cameron's photographs.

Grove described the history of the collection from 1852 onwards and some of the daily procedures of its management. The first reference that he had been able to find to a Photographs Section in the Art Library was in 1864. He wrote of the rationale of the collection. His statement recognizes an expansion beyond the representation of works of art:

> The collection, being intended for the use of all varieties of workers – manufacturers, teachers, art students, pattern designers, and workers in the various trades and crafts – naturally includes photographs of many objects besides those which belong to the fine arts or to the industrial arts. A use is indeed found for photographs of almost every kind of object; the plant, flower, and animal studies are in constant use by designers and book illustrators, while architectural and topographical views become of value as records, and are used by many readers in addition to those who are students of architecture.The collection includes examples of almost every kind of photographic reproduction, and in this manner it illustrates the history of the art of photography.[1]

Grove viewed the Photography Collection as a visual encyclopaedia, forming a history of the art of photography as a significant by-product, but essentially at the service of all comers.

No wonder Grove responded favourably when a M. Eugène Atget wrote to the Museum on 19 November 1902. The Parisian photographer offered prints for sale from an impressive inventory. His speciality was *Le Vieux Paris*:

1 Les Hôtels particuliers
2 Les Maisons historiques ou curieuses
3 Aspects et Vieilles rues
4 {Les quais, les ponts, les Ports, Les Marchés, Squares et Jardins
5 Fontaines et Puits
6 Les Portes Artistiques (Boiseries)
7 Heurtoirs et Mascarons
8 Escaliers (bois et fer forgé) (maison particulière)
9 Les Enseignes – Boutiques et Cabarets
1000 clichés (à suivre)
10 Types et petits métiers de la Rue (200 clichés)[2]

The letter also offered *Les Petits Environs de Paris* and Atget trailed, with much vigorous underlining, a new series, still in preparation, on *Les grands Environs de Paris*.

M. Atget's photographs of Paris shop-fronts (Plate 48) were bought for one franc each in 1903. Views taken outside Paris were offered at 1 franc 50 centimes, which the Museum negotiated down to 1 franc 25. Altogether, 572 photographs were bought from Atget in the period 1903–05. The Museum took the trouble to write to Atget in French until November 1905. Thereafter there were, perhaps coincidentally, no more offers of prints. However, Grove thought his prices high and that another Paris photographer, called Leroy, might be just as good and cost less.

Atget's story has become a potent myth. His work was taken up by Man Ray, who lived in the same street in the 1920s. Atget's photograph *L'Eclipse – avril 1912*, showing a group of Parisians gazing blindly at the sun, was used on the cover of *La Révolution Surréaliste* on 26 June 1926. It was used with Atget's reluctant permission, and on condition that he was not credited. His photograph was wittily re-captioned *Les Derniers Conversions*. Atget insisted that he was not an art photographer, that he simply made 'documents' for artists. The remarkable qualities of his documentary photographs were to convert many photographers to the cause of 'straight' photography – and to its subtleties. His work inspired the young American Berenice Abbott, who saved a vast collection of Atget's prints, negatives and memorabilia for posterity. The achievement is enshrined in four exemplary volumes, written by John Szarkowski and Maria Morris Hambourg, published by The Museum of Modern Art, New York, between 1981 and 1985. Maria Morris Hambourg pointed out that the ironwork which embellished hostelries was a legal requirement: 'Because they served alcohol and were open at night, the bistros, cabarets, and inns of Old Paris had been required by law to be fenced round with strong iron grilles. The only unbarred

48. Eugène Atget (French, 1857–1927). **Paris, 62 rue de l'Hôtel de Ville**. Albumen print. 8½ × 6¾ in (21.7 × 17.3 cm). Bought from the photographer, 1903. 2204–1903.

PLATS

opening was the door through which clients entered or else handed in a container to be filled'.[3] More recently, Molly Nesbit has returned us to Atget's sense of his photographs as documents, absolutely intended for the role they found in such archives as the V&A's.[4]

Atget was one of the last photographers to use the albumen process for his prints. Grove asked him to quote prices for prints in the more permanent platinum process, but Atget replied that he did not know how to print in platinum. By 1900 most photographers were using gelatin-based papers. These were typically development papers, exposed briefly under a negative and then chemically developed, producing the black-and-white print typical of the twentieth century. Gelatin papers containing silver bromide came into general use about 1880 and continue to be used today. Atget was also among the last photographers to make his living by selling his photographic prints to archives. Nesbit suggests that he conceived his work as a series of seven albums, which he hoped would become printed books. Already by the time he died in 1927 a revolution in high-speed ink printing had occurred. From the 1920s to the 1970s most photographers looked primarily to the printed pages of magazines and books for their audiences and markets. Atget's first book was posthumous. *Atget: Photographe de Paris* was published in 1930. It became one of the most influential photographic books of the century. The pattern shifted, slowly and not at all completely, from buying photographic prints to buying photographs printed in halftones. The compact, illustrated book was to the portfolio or filing cabinet of photographs (or any other kind of prints, any other kind of art) as the CD-ROM is now becoming to certain kinds of large-scale illustrated book.

Man Ray made fine prints like his portrait of Meret Oppenheim (Plate 49) for presentation to his friends, in this case to Oppenheim herself. The print is inscribed to her. He also made prints for occasional exhibitions. However, his principal vehicles as a photographer were the book, notably *Man Ray: Photographs 1920–34* (1934), and magazines. He crossed back and forth from Surrealist high art to Surrealist high fashion in the welcoming pages of *Harper's Bazaar*. Man Ray's portrait of his fellow-Surrealist Meret Oppenheim used the technique of solarization, the Sabattier effect, to combine the positive and the negative simultaneously. Oppenheim's whiplash profile is as metallic and moderne as any streamlined goddess on the bonnet of a Bugatti.

The discovery of solarization as a usable, indeed the perfect, Surrealist technique, was made in Man Ray's studio by his lover and apprentice Lee Miller:

> Something crawled across my foot in the darkroom and I let out a yell and turned on the light. I never did find out what it was, a mouse or what. Then I realized that the film was totally exposed: there in the development tanks, ready to be taken out, were a dozen practically fully developed negatives of a nude against a black background. Man Ray grabbed them, put them in the hypo and looked at

49. MAN RAY (American, 1890–1976). **Portrait of Meret Oppenheim**, 1933. Solarized gelatin-silver print. 11¾ × 8⅝ in (30 × 22 cm). Bought 1984. Ph.68–1984.

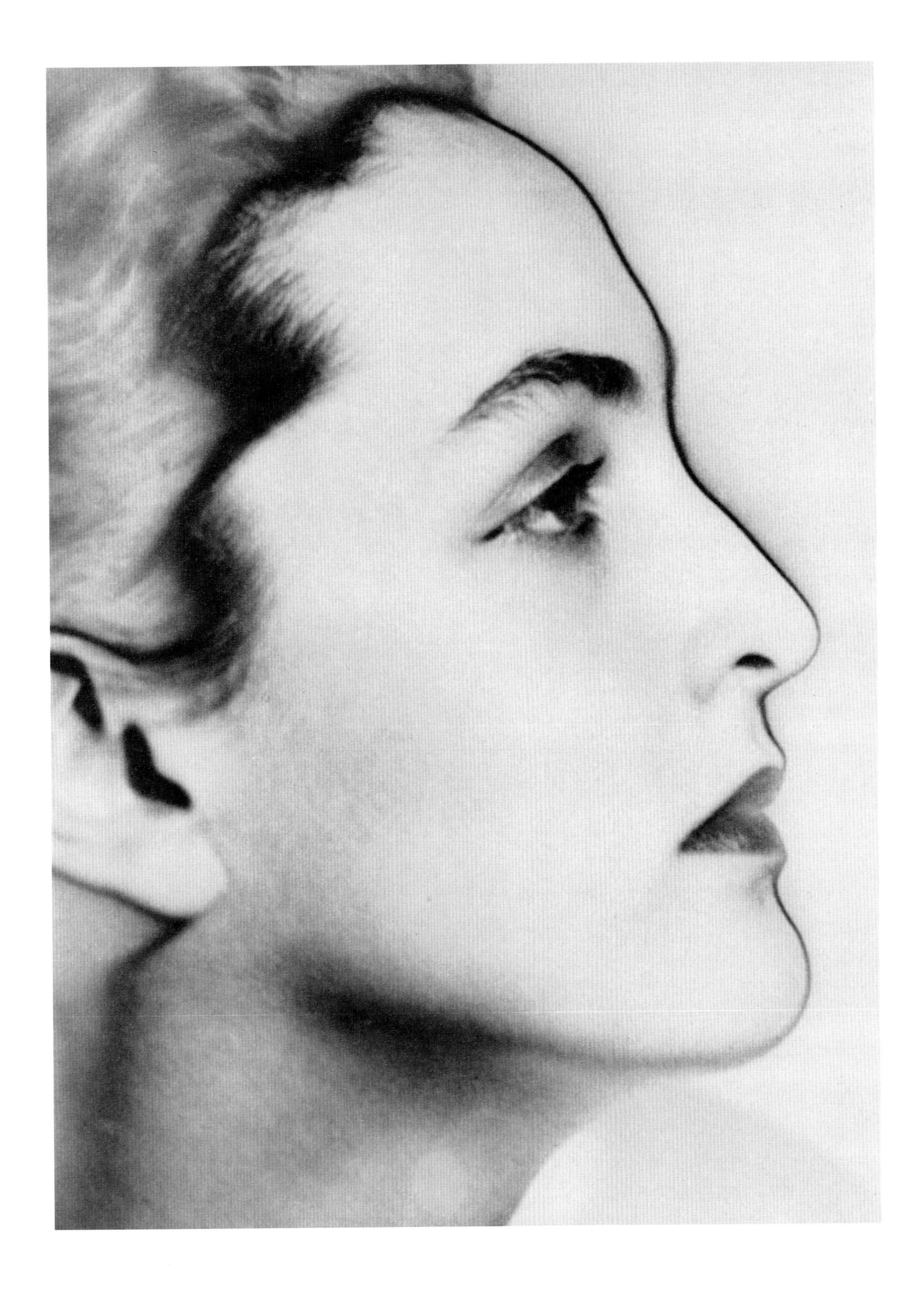

50. LEE MILLER (British, born United States, 1907–77). **The Exploding Hand**, 1930. Gelatin-silver print. 9⅜ × 11¾ in (23.7 × 30 cm). Bought 1984. Ph.101–1984.

> them: the unexposed parts of the negative, which had been the black background, had been exposed by this sharp light that had been turned on and they had developed and came right up to the edge of the white nude body... It was all very well my making that one accidental discovery, but then Man had to set about how to control it and make it come out exactly the way he wanted to each time.[5]

Lee Miller herself became an imaginative photographer. Her most famous photograph came to the V&A collection much later (1984) from her family, who have put her archive meticulously in order. Miller's Paris shop-door, titled *The Exploding Hand* (Plate 50), belongs to the world that replaced Atget's – that of Surrealism and 'convulsive beauty'.

Lee Miller also crossed over from the roles of photographic artist and artist's model – the inspiration of some of Man Ray's greatest masterpieces – to become a fashion model and photojournalist. The fashions of the independent new woman became her particularly well (Plate 51). Lee Miller became part of the new wave of women photojournalists. She took her Surrealism into the battle zone as one of the most able and distinguished photojournalists of the Second World War.

Man Ray and Miller were among countless artist-immigrants to Paris in the 'Twenties. Major photographers included Brassai from Transylvania and André Kertesz from Budapest. George Hoyningen-Huene, who photographed Lee Miller for *Vogue*, was born in St Petersburg and moved on from Paris to New York. The Berliner Marianne Breslauer was another member of Man Ray's circle. Like other remarkable women of the time, she adopted photography and the light, new cameras of the time – typified by the Leica, introduced in 1925 – to look at the world from unexpected vantage points. Apart from her fascinating gallery of portraits, Breslauer made an abstract street pattern above the café La Rotonde in Paris in 1929 (Plate 52). Such viewpoints, with their slanting perspectives and startling shadows, became part of an international style in the late 'Twenties. Highly graphic photographs suited the new illustrated magazines, like *Vu* in Paris, and other commercial applications. Breslauer's Paris scene was used as a cover for the book *Begegnungen* ('Meetings') by Gotthard Jedlicka, published in Basel in 1933. Although Breslauer published this photograph in a late monograph of her work as it appears here, an old pencil inscription shows that at one time it was viewed the other way up – which emphasizes the Surrealist nature of the image.[6]

Berlin was another cosmopolitan centre of the period. El Lissitzky moved there from Moscow in 1922. He met Van Doesburg, a fellow Constructivist, Schwitters, the Dadaist and the innovatory artist-designer Herbert Bayer. El Lissitzky experimented with photo-collages, printing from a 'sandwich' of two negatives, and printing on to paper tilted under the enlarger. He used this to stretch and dramatize the forms of products for advertising, as in the advertisement for Pelikan ink made in

Berlin in 1924 (Plate 53). Cosmopolitanism was not confined to the German capital: it was part of the essential atmosphere of Europe's most experimental art school, the Bauhaus. Its founding director Walter Gropius was impressively, even definitively, photographed in 1929 (Plate 54) by Hugo Erfurth, a Photo-Secessionist who had modernized his style. Edward Steichen did the same, forsaking the salons of the Secession to become chief photographer at Condé Nast, New York (*Vogue* and *Vanity Fair*), in 1923. Herbert Bayer was among the students at the Weimar Bauhaus. Gropius brought him back as a teacher, at Dessau, in 1925–8. *Metamorphosis*, Bayer's photo-collage or 'photo-plastik' from 1936, perfectly evokes the vigorously experimental and Utopian Bauhaus spirit (Plate 55).

51. George Hoyningen-Huene (Russian, 1900–68). **Lee Miller Wearing Yraide Sailcloth Overalls**, 1930. Gelatin-silver print. 9⅜ × 7 in (24 × 18 cm). Bought 1984. Ph.102–1984.

That spirit quickly became the focus of international admiration. However, there was little or no market for photographic prints as collectors' items at the time. By contrast, there was a thriving market for contemporary etchings and drypoint prints – indeed, it amounted to a 'print boom' during the 1920s and 1930s.[7] The important market for photographers was now in selling reproduction rights. Apart from the framed portrait or passport photograph, and a number of documentary/technical applications, the fundamental role of photographic prints at this period was to be translated into halftone printing plates. Because photographs as prints usually had no other role, it sometimes proved difficult to assign them a financial value.

The English painter (Sir) Roland Penrose and other artists in London arranged an exhibition in support of the Left during the Spanish Civil War. Penrose went to Paris for pictures, and to the flat of the great photojournalist Robert Capa. The transaction that followed exemplifies the lack of market value for photographic prints, if in a unique and bizarre form. Penrose remembered it all his life and recounted it to the present writer in the early 1980s. The tale was recently confirmed by Antony Penrose, who tells it as follows:

> Capa was away, but his mother, who Roland described as being elderly, rather deaf and speaking very little French, got out the photos for him to see. After a careful deliberation he made his choice, and asked how much they cost. Capa's mother did not have a clue how much to charge, and things got very complicated until she was struck with an idea. She scuttled off into a back room and returned carrying the kind of balance scales which peasant people used in country markets and demanded to know how much a kilo Roland was offering. She was clearly prepared to haggle. Roland was absolutely astonished, but he solved the problem by leaving the amount he thought correct and departed, with instructions for Capa to contact him if there was a discrepancy. He said that after that whenever he met Capa it was a running gag between them – and Capa would greet Roland with: 'Here's the man who tried to buy my photos by the kilo – so how much are you offering today then?'[8]

TAPIS

52. Marianne Breslauer (Swiss, born Berlin 1909). **Paris**, 1929. Gelatin-silver print. 9⅛ × 6¾ in (23.2 × 17.2 cm). Given by the photographer in memory of Arthur and Tamara Kauffmann, 1984. Ph.797–1987.

(right)
Figure 8. Laszlo Moholy-Nagy (American, born Hungary, 1895–1946). **14 Bauhaus Books**, *c.*1928. Illustration from eight-page photographic brochure printed in red and black on art paper. 5⅞ × 8¼ in (14.7 × 21 cm). Published by Albert Langen, Munich. S891001, JP Box 226. National Art Library, V&A.

During the modern period – say 1920–60 – the Photography Collection did not, therefore, acquire the art of photography in the form of gelatin-silver prints. Much of the collecting focus was, as in the Museum as a whole, on collecting Englishness: photographs of churches, stained glass, sculpture, ancient buildings. However, the Museum did collect modern photography in an unusually potent form, as Jeremy Aynsley has recently reminded us.[9]

In the 1930s Philip James, the Museum's Librarian, initiated a collection of modern commercial typography. He organized a whole exhibition on the subject in 1936. In the catalogue of *Modern Commercial Typography* James particularly thanked Herbert Bayer for helping to collect material for the show. Bayer himself was represented by some Bauhaus work, furniture brochures and a printer's sample of the Univers type of 1926. This was the lower-case alphabet intended for use in all Bauhaus literature. Photography was among the fifteen sections of the exhibition. James noted that 'continental jobbing printing responds far more quickly to current movements in art and design than does the work in this country'.[10] Others with an impact on the collection were Jan Tschichold and Laszlo Moholy-Nagy (Figure 8). Nazi outrages had already brought Moholy-Nagy and Gropius briefly to London before they moved on to the United States. As Aynsley points out, the Moholy-Nagy brochure for Bauhaus books followed Constructivist ideas by using the components of

TINTE

53. El Lissitzky (Eliezer Markovich) (Russian, 1890–1941). **Pelikan Tinte**, 1924. Gelatin-silver print. 5¾ × 4 in (14.5 × 10 cm). Ph.143–1985.

typography to convey its message. The line of type was transposed as printed characters and then re-photographed.

Other talents had moved away from the salons of art photography to seek more urgent issues and address a more populous mainstream. Paul Strand was first published and exhibited by Alfred Stieglitz in New York in 1916–17. He remained under the influence of the Stieglitz circle until 1932. He brought the subtle tonal values of high pictorialism into the high modernism of the 'Twenties and 'Thirties. The rich tonal resonance and exquisite craftsmanship of Strand's negatives had a compelling influence on his younger contemporary Ansel Adams, who saw them in Taos, New Mexico in 1930. The values that so impressed Adams can be seen in Strand's image of *Church, Ranchos de Taos, New Mexico* (Plate 56).

Strand moved soon afterwards into socialism and cinema. His superb film *Redes* ('The Wave') was made for the Mexican Secretariat of Education in 1934. Other films followed. Thereafter Strand's contribution as a photographer was seen in an exemplary and influential series of books, always published with important texts. They began with *Time in New England* (1950) and continued with *La France du Profil* (1952), *Un Paese* (1955), *Tir a'Mhurain* (on the Hebridean island of South Uist, 1962), *Living Egypt* (1969) and finally *Ghana: An African Portrait* (1975). The first Strand prints to enter the Photography Collection were acquired, as we shall see, in 1975.

Cosmopolitanism is even more marked in the career of Emil Otto Hoppé. Born in Munich in 1878, Hoppé became the leading portrait photographer in Edwardian London. He took on the palatial studio of Sir John Millais in South Kensington, where he made platinum portraits of the literary lions of the day. He photographed a pantheon, from the Anglo-American Henry James, to the Anglo-Indian Rudyard Kipling. He photographed the stars of London's theatre and Diaghilev's Ballets Russes. He designed for the theatre himself, was art editor of the magazine *Colour* and performed with astute professionalism in the new field of advertising photography.[11] He went to New York to photograph for his *Book of Fair Women* (1922) and to promote himself. Crucially, he began to publish his portraits in the picture press, where his work was ardently admired by the celebrity photographer who became his natural successor. Cecil Beaton grew up on Hoppé portraiture in the magazines. He recalled in 1945 that 'when these reproductions were placed in a sort of magic lantern that I possessed, and enlarged to gargantuan proportions on the wall, the effect was almost overwhelming'.[12]

In 1925 Hoppé abandoned the studio for the roving life of a travel photographer-cum-photojournalist. He published a series of hefty volumes, beginning with a tour across the United States. *Key West, Florida* (Plate 57) captures the thrill of Hoppé's new career – and that of hundreds of travelling photographers like him. The nineteenth-century study of the instantaneous became, in the twentieth century, a universal drama of speed. There was a headlong rush to see, photograph and publish

54. Hugo Erfurth (German, 1874–1948). **Portrait of Walter Gropius**, 1928. Gelatin-silver print. 11¼ × 9 in (28.8 × 23 cm). Bought 1987. Ph.796–1987.

everything, apparently, in the world. Hoppé travelled as photo-reporter in Europe – especially Germany – the United States, India, Indonesia, Japan and Australia. Sometimes finesse got lost in the chase. His fabulously well timed and framed *Key West* photograph is an unpublished variant, rather better than the two related photographs chosen for his American book. This appeared in London as *The United States of America* and in New York as *Romantic America: Picturesque United States* (1927). Although Hoppé's studio was less than five minutes from the V&A, and although he photographed extensively in the Museum in 1931, his prints were not acquired for the Photography Collection in his (exceptionally long) life time. He died in 1972.

Although he held exhibitions, Hoppé's world – after his initial portrait period – was that of books, magazines and reproduction rights. In 1939 he transformed himself again. He founded the Dorien Leigh photography agency in London in 1939. His career became a collection of images, a resource, a photo-library for the picture press and for book publishing, a cosmopolitan archive. Subsequently parts of Hoppé's archive joined the Mansell Collection, a commercial picture library, and other parts passed to his descendants. It has been largely reconstituted by Graham Howe during the 1990s as the E.O. Hoppé Archive in Pasadena, California. It is very much in Hoppé's spirit that the archive of his photographs is currently being digitized for global access and commercial distribution in the electronic age.

Charles Harvard Gibbs-Smith (1909–82), who succeeded T.C. Grove, was in charge of the Photography Collection in the 1930s. Grove published nothing on the Photography Collection and it seems an apt reflection of his photographic interests that in retirement he co-wrote the history (many times reprinted) of a local parish church. Gibbs-Smith was communicative and publicity minded, at least in the context of the Museum ethos of the time. He wrote of photography's new age when he introduced *Victorian Snapshots* by Paul Martin in 1939. Two years earlier he had borrowed negatives from Martin and had enlargements made in the Museum's studio for the Photography Collection. (The negatives were later bought by Helmut Gernsheim, with many other Paul Martin items, and are now part of the Gernsheim Collection in the Harry Ransom Research Center for the Humanities at the University of Texas, Austin.) Because of the Museum regulations of the day, Gibbs-Smith published his introduction to *Victorian Snapshots* under the name of 'Charles Harvard':

> A century ago the world's mind came to be fitted with a new pictorial lining. Until the third decade of the nineteenth century the memory was fed from the real world of people and things and supported by the flat world of pictures and prints. It must have been a very colourful affair which allowed the imagination to make its way unhindered and encouraged poetical imagery to suggest an inexhaustible world of fantasy.
>
> Then came photography. And, ever since, we have come to think more and

55. Herbert Bayer (American, born Austria, 1900–85). **Metamorphosis**, 1936. Gelatin-silver print. 10 × 13⅜ in (25.4 × 34 cm). Bought from the photographer, 1969. Circ.652–1969.

> more in terms of drab, monochrome images. An accurate and uncompromising supply of photographic knowledge is continually poured into our minds. We are fed on photographs daily until we die. They meet us on hoardings, in shops, in newspapers, in books, in our work and in many of our amusements. Behind the scenes of everyday life they have spread in their applications until there is scarcely a department of science and industry that does not employ them. Photography has not only helped the modern eclipse of time and space, but brought about a revolution in thinking and (for good or evil) transported the world to our doorsteps.[13]

When he wrote of photography's global reach, Gibbs-Smith was not just reciting platitudes. He had recently overseen the registration in the Photography Collection of just such a world-shrinking archive. It arrived at the V&A by courtesy of The Museum of Modern Art (MoMA) in New York. There were cordial relations between MoMA's founding Director Alfred J. Barr, and the V&A's Director Sir Eric Maclagan. In 1932–3 the V&A had bought two sets of a portfolio of colour plates of Diego Rivera murals, one for the Library and one for the Circulation Department. In 1934 it bought a set of 509 photographs which recorded MoMA's International Exhibition of Theatre Arts. MoMA planned a similar corpus of photographs as a record of its landmark show *African Negro Sculpture* in 1935. Gibbs-Smith reserved a set at once.

The exhibition was an act of homage and of popularization. It was built on the perceptions of the avant-garde artists, in Dresden and Paris, who had recognized the vitality of African sculpture from around 1905. Ethnographic items had become sculpture and, as the exhibition's curator James Johnson Sweeney wrote: 'As a sculptural tradition in the last century it has had no rivals. It is as sculpture we should approach it'.[14] MoMA received funding from the US General Education Board to commission a photographic 'corpus' of many of the exhibits temporarily gathered in New York, and to distribute these at nominal cost to five museums and selected educational institutions. Part of the point was to provide sets to black colleges in the United States. MoMA's executive director Thomas Dabney Mabry Jr wrote to Maclagan about the project on 20 November 1935: 'Walker Evans, the well-known photographer, has spent months making these photographs and the result, in my opinion, is unsurpassed in contemporary photography' (Figure 9). Evans had photographed some of the exhibits many times over. In May 1936 the V&A received the set of 477 unmounted photographs at a total price of $50. Sets were distributed free to Atlanta University, Atlanta, Georgia; Fisk University, Nashville, Tennessee; Hampton Institute, Hampton, Virginia; Tuskegee Normal and Industrial Institute, Tuskegee, Alabama; Howard University, Washington, DC; Dillard University, New Orleans, Louisiana; and the New York Public Library.[15]

Walker Evans had discovered African sculpture as a young man in Paris in the

Figure 9. WALKER EVANS (American, 1903–75). **Ancestral Figure, Gabun, Ogowe River, Bakota**, 1936. Gelatin-silver print. Bought from The Museum of Modern Art, New York, 1936. 8¹¹/₁₆ × 5¾ in (22.1 × 14.7 cm). 2321–1936.

'Twenties, when he had also discovered the photography of Eugène Atget. This great documentary project involved Evans and his assistants in countless sessions, working with the exhibits out of Museum hours, and the production of 8,000 prints. He used one fixed light source and a second one in motion. He interpreted the exhibits as sculptures, glistening with cosmopolitan modernity.

Gibbs-Smith's introduction to *Victorian Snapshots*, quoted above, sounds ambivalent. It almost presages the disenchantment of Susan Sontag's *On Photography* (1979). In another article, again published under a pseudonym, Gibbs-Smith was more optimistic and this time he anticipates the Steichen of *The Family of Man* (1955) – or an Internet enthusiast. He wrote '100 Years of Photography' for a special supplement to *John O'London's Weekly* on 2 December 1938:

> The power for general good inherent in the whole field and achievements of photography is immense. There can never be too much information or too many facts in the world. Misuse of them will diminish as they increase and become broadcast, and in this service the camera is, perhaps, only second to the printed word. Like the telegraph, telephone, and wireless, photography makes for the diminution of distance, for the unification of peoples of the earth as step by step the hoard of our knowledge becomes the common property of everyone. Romantics see this as a tragedy; realists find in it hope for ultimate world fraternity.

At the end of the article Gibbs-Smith turned to collecting:

> Practically nobody takes the trouble to collect old photographs, and yet the time has already come when they are *objets d'art.* The work to look out for is that done before about 1860, together with the few outstanding examples of later years...

Gibbs-Smith organized a modest but significant *Exhibition of Early Photographs to Commemorate the Centenary of Photography, 1839–1939*. Cannily – he was to become the Museum's head of public relations – Gibbs-Smith arranged that it should open on 25 January 1939, exactly 100 years after Talbot's invention was first publicly announced by Michael Faraday at the Royal Institution. Some 20 press photographs were produced to publicize the exhibition. They were widely reproduced in the press, but had a greater importance. The newly taken copy negatives of some of the Museum's greatest photographs became part of the Picture Library stock. They were conveniently available for historians and other writers.

Lucia Moholy made good use of these photographs in her paperback *A Hundred Years of Photography* published by Penguin Books in 1939. It was a topical 'Pelican Special', a series that included *The New German Empire*, *Microbes by the Million* and *Poland*. She illustrated Watson's nude (Plate 14), Camille Silvy's *River Scene, France*, plus works by Fenton, Cameron and Muybridge. Mrs Cameron's *St Agnes* (acquired in

56. Paul Strand (American, 1890–1976). **Santa Ana Mission, Santa Ana Pueblo, New Mexico**, 1930–2. Platinum print. 4¾ × 5⅞ in (12 × 15 cm). Given by the Paul Strand Foundation in memory of Gordon Fraser. Ph.400–1983.

1865) appeared in *Lilliput* magazine for March 1939, along with *Egeria*. They appeared with the title 'The Art of Margaret Cameron' (*sic*), plus this detail about *Egeria*: 'A recent acquisition of the Victoria and Albert Museum, this is the first reproduction since its re-discovery'.

Anniversaries often produce a flurry of activity and enthusiasm. Although photographers had constantly discussed the matter in the late nineteenth century – when the Art Library remained oblivious – it had at last become clear to the Museum that photography had accumulated a serious history. By the 1930s the works of the pioneers had passed down to children and grandchildren. Archives had to be dealt with. Although photographica still had no financial value, they possessed every other kind. Miss Matilda Talbot OBE made one of the greatest of all donations to any museum in 1937. She presented her grandfather's cameras, plus thousands of negatives and prints, to the Science Museum. These are now among the great treasures of the National Museum of Photography, Film and Television, Bradford, founded in 1983.

The first of the modern histories was about to be written. At MoMA Beaumont Newhall, the young librarian, researched and produced the exhibition *The History of Photography from 1839 to the Present* (1937). His exhibition catalogue became a book that has been reprinted and revised many times. Newhall became the founding director of MoMA's Department of Photography in 1940.

Gibbs-Smith took advantage of the centenary too. As the Museum had no copy of *The Pencil of Nature*, he advertised for it in the trade. It was offered at a guinea or two, even then a ludicrously low price. Gibbs-Smith consulted his conscience and then Sir Eric Maclagan – who told him to buy, on the principle that the transactions between museums and dealers even themselves out over time.[16] Perhaps Gibbs-Smith, or his exhibition, encouraged the gift of the Frederick Hollyer albums. They arrived in 1938 and took an honoured place in his show, with copy prints on the wall and the albums open in desk-cases. Many key works by Cameron were given by Miss Perrin in 1939. Also in 1939, Miss E.M. Spiller, art lecturer at the Museum, donated Claudet's portrait of Andrew Pritchard (Plate 4) and J.L. Nevinson of the Department of Textiles and Dress gave a series of Kilburn Daguerreotypes (see Plate 9). These were also exhibited, and much illustrated in the press.

One of the visitors drawn to the exhibition by the considerable press attention was Lady Clementina Tottenham, granddaughter of Lady Hawarden. She sought out Gibbs-Smith to ask why the photographs by her pioneering grandmother had not been included in the show. Gibbs-Smith replied that unfortunately the Photography Collection possessed none of Lady Hawarden's works. Lady Clementina then gave the Museum 775 photographs. It was among the most important gifts of photographs ever received by the Museum and has already been referred to in chapter four. The Horatio Ross Daguerreotype in Plate 5, and seven others, may also have been given –

57. EMIL OTTO HOPPÉ (British, born Germany, 1878–1972). **Key West, Florida**, 1926. Gelatin-silver print. 6⅝ × 8½ in (16.8 × 22 cm). Given by Graham Howe, 1996. E.629–1996.

by a Major Ross – in 1939, although they were not officially registered until 1946.

Any further impetus that might have been generated by the 1939 exhibition was lost when first the threat and then the actuality of the Second World War intervened. At the end of the 1930s the V&A had recognized the value of early photographs as *objets d'art* and begun to collect (at least in the case of Talbot) proactively. The Art Library subscribed to such annuals as the English *Modern Photography* and *Photographie*, published by Arts et Métiers Graphiques in Paris. Important books were acquired from New York, such as the first edition of Beaumont Newhall's history and of Walker Evans's *American Photographs* (published by MoMA in 1938). It is somewhat startling to find Gibbs-Smith writing in 1939 that Paul Martin 'ranks with Stieglitz in America and Atget in Paris, both of whom he preceded, and with whom he forms the vanguard of the great moderns'.[17] In practical terms, the Museum bought no works by Atget or Stieglitz in the 1930s, not even Atget's posthumous book, and acquired no prints by Paul Martin, except the new gelatin-silver prints from his negatives made in its own studio. We cannot even be sure that Gibbs-Smith was aware that the Museum owned hundreds of prints by Atget. These were not signed or identified as by Atget on the mounts and were filed under subject (such as, 'Decorative Ironwork' or a place name). Many had been transferred to other departments, probably as a result of the Report of the Committee of Re-Arrangement of 1908. The European avant-garde came to the Museum, as we have seen, in the form of the jobbing printing collection gathered by Philip James. The Museum seems to have held the same position as the *News Chronicle*, which greeted the Early Photographs show on 25 January 1939: 'Photography's Own Old Masters are Victorian / ART MODERNS CANNOT BEAT'. Apart from the special case of its early stars, like Talbot, Claudet, Kilburn, Hawarden, Cameron, Hollyer and Martin, photography was collected because it was functional. Another review of the 1939 show reminds us that there was much for photography to be functional about. 'Snapshots of History' by 'The Man In The Street' appeared in the *Star*, a London newspaper, on 25 January 1939:

> Looking through the national service list of reserved occupations, I see that it includes photographers.
>
> So, by a highly dramatic accident, the seal is set on the vast importance of Fox Talbot's invention *one hundred years to the very day after it was disclosed*.
>
> If there is another war, photographers will be key men, their work a vital medium of propaganda and information.
>
> Yet it all began as a charming toy.

Those in 'reserved occupations' were not automatically conscripted into the armed services. After the war came, the British Ministry of Information looked around to find a photographer for a particularly important assignment. In 1940 German bombing raids on London became severe. The population fled at night into the relative safety

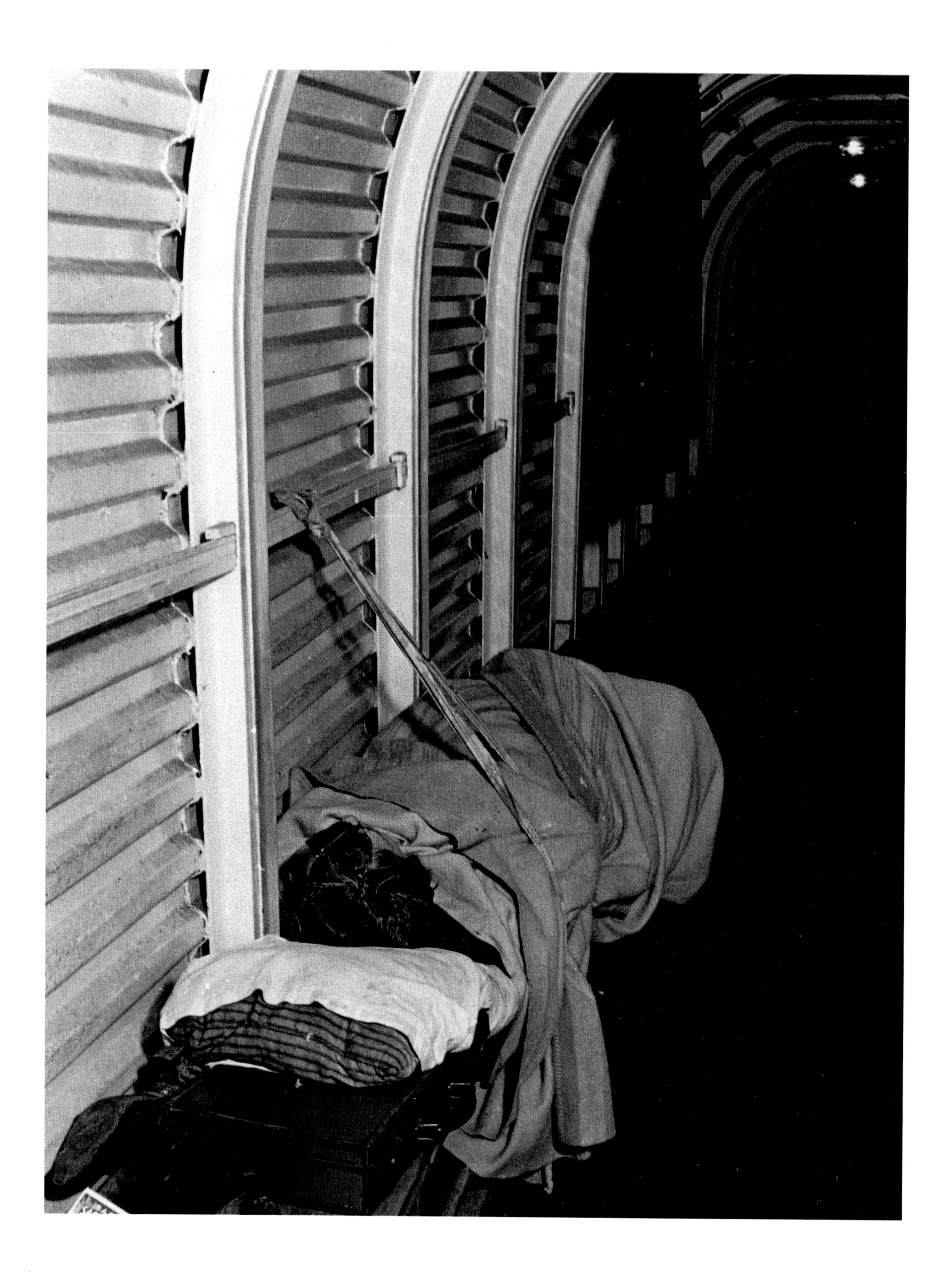

Figure 10. BILL BRANDT (British, 1904–83). **North London Air Raid Shelter**, 1940. Gelatin-silver print. 10 × 7⅞ in (25.3 × 20 cm). Given by Sir Fife Clark, 1980. Ph.1193–1980.

of the Underground stations. The authorities turned the platforms into air-raid shelters. Britain's survival hung in the balance – but the United States maintained its neutrality. It was thought that photographs of Londoners enduring the Blitz might help win over American hearts and minds. The Ministry of Information made an obvious but still inspired choice of photographer.

Bill Brandt (1904–83) could hardly have been more cosmopolitan. He was born in Hamburg of an English father and German mother. He had spent his teenage years convalescing in Davos, Switzerland. Brandt found his vocation and his first – Hungarian – wife in Vienna, where the American poet Ezra Pound offered him an introduction to Man Ray in Paris. Brandt studied with Man Ray in the late 1920s. He discovered the worlds of Surrealism and of Atget – then married in Barcelona, settled in London in 1931 and became Britain's most admired photojournalist. Night scenes were one of his specialities. Perhaps the image in Figure 10 owes something to both Atget and Surrealism. It owes even more to the flash bulb introduced in the late 1920s. Unlike earlier unpredictable, smoky and sometimes dangerous methods, the flashbulb was relatively discreet. The left foreground shows a piece of publicity for the 'Baby Sashalite' flash favoured by Brandt and his friend Brassai. During an official visit to Britain in late 1940 Wendell Wilkie, an opponent of United States involvement in the war, was given a complete set of Brandt's shelter photographs to take back to President Roosevelt. A selection from the series was given to the Museum in 1980 by Sir Fife Clark, who served during the war as Public Relations Officer of the Ministry of Health (which was responsible for health conditions in the shelters). He thought that Brandt's photographs undoubtedly influenced United States policy on aid for embattled Britain.[18] However, like much else, the initiatives in photography at the V&A by Philip James and Charles Gibbs-Smith came to an end for the duration of the war and through its long aftermath.

CHAPTER SIX

BEING CONTEMPORARY

THE SECOND WORLD WAR changed Britain in every dimension, lowering – if not levelling – class barriers and etching itself everywhere. The Museum's splintered masonry on Exhibition Road bears witness to wartime bombing. Because damage to the Tate Gallery was still being repaired, immediately after the war, the V&A held a spectacular exhibition of Picasso and Matisse. Fifty works, mainly recent and lent by the artists, drew a large audience to the otherwise empty Museum when it reopened in 1945. The collections, evacuated to deep caves in Wales for the duration, began to return and the galleries to be transformed. The energetic Director Sir Leigh Ashton envisaged a more dynamic and comprehensible display. He laid out the Museum's 'Primary' galleries (now called Art and Design galleries), which bring together masterpieces in art and design from each major period. These are complemented by 'Secondary' (now called Processes and Techniques) galleries, which both expressed and furthered the Museum's world-class connoisseurship in the areas that it collected. The Museum's attitude to collecting photographs was also to be transformed in the decades after the war – but not immediately.

Lucia Moholy's *A Hundred Years of Photography* (1939), mentioned in the last chapter, was a complex, up-to-date and lyrical view of the medium. A quotation from Daumier appeared on the title page: 'Je suis de mon temps' ('I am of my time'). Moholy's final paragraph celebrates photography's astonishing development 'from its early beginnings as a kind of magic art, one hundred years ago, to the status of a world power which it has now reached. Life without photographs is no longer imaginable. They pass before our eyes and awaken our interest; they pass through the atmosphere unseen and unheard, over distances of thousands of miles. They are in our lives, as our lives are in them.'[1] Moholy was thinking of such phenomena as photo-telegraphy – used since the 1920s – but her rhapsody also evokes an even newer medium. Television transmissions, moving photos flying through the air, had hesitantly begun in London in 1936. Perhaps television provides one of the keys to understanding the profound change in attitudes to photography as an artistic medium that occurred between 1951 and 1964.

The direct consequences of the Second World War – chaos, shortages, rationing and general depression – were felt until 1951. Conditions in much of continental Europe were, of course, far more severe. Surprisingly, the first post-war international movement in creative photography began at Saarbrucken, just inside the German

58. WOLFGANG REISEWITZ (German, born 1917). **Glockenzug**, 1949. Gelatin-silver print. 15 × 10⅛ in (38 × 25.6 cm). Bought from Roger Mayne, 1985. Ph.309–1985.

border with France. There Dr Otto Steinert launched a series of exhibitions and books under the title *Subjektive Fotografie*. 'Subjective' meant free, personal, non-functional practice. Among the cold realities following Year Zero, Steinert tried to revive the experimental spirit of Man Ray, Moholy-Nagy and the Bauhaus.

One of the movement's most characteristic productions is *Glockenzug* ('Hanging the Bells') by Wolfgang Reisewitz (Plate 58). It captures a very particular moment in European and photographic history. The bells of the thirteenth-century Evangelical Stiftskirche in Neustadt, in the Rheinland-Pfalz, had been melted down for munitions in the war. The photograph shows new bells being raised, watched by townspeople, in 1949. This complex image is a negative print of a photomontage. How was it made? At five in the afternoon (the clock on the tower had stopped), Reisewitz photographed a bell being raised at the side of the church. He made a second exposure from the same position ten minutes later. He placed the two negatives side by side, one of them flipped over, copied them on to transparency film and finally produced a negative enlargement. Reisewitz and others of his generation saw photography as a seamless blending of reality and fantasy. His picture makes a half real, half imaginary space in which the new bells are lifted into the post-war world. *Glockenzug* was widely exhibited in the 1950s, but was not bought at the time by the Museum. This print was acquired by the young British photographer Roger Mayne, who participated in *Subjektive Fotografie* exhibitions and worked to accomplish something similar in Britain. The Museum bought this and other photographs, including two by Steinert, from Mayne in 1985.

The Festival of Britain in 1951 commemorated, of course, 1851. It was a nationwide series of events, intended as 'A Tonic To the Nation', marking the end of 'Aftermath' and ushering in better times. The V&A participated by presenting *Masterpieces of Victorian Photography* from the collection of Helmut and Alison Gernsheim, who had begun collecting in 1945. The show was proposed to the Museum by its former Librarian, Philip James, who had become Director of Art at the newly created Arts Council of Great Britain.[2] It was shown in the Octagon Gallery (Room 49), right at the front of the Museum, under its imposing central tower. The installation was painted deep red, a sympathetic and appropriate colour for Victorian photographs. Although by then in charge of public relations, or 'Extension Services' as they were called, Gibbs-Smith worked with Helmut Gernsheim on the practicalities of the exhibition. Presentation was basic. The photographs were covered by glass and only the smaller ones were mounted. Royal College of Art students hung the show. In homage to 1851 they displayed, 'stained-glass style' (that is, with light shining from behind), a large paper negative of the Crystal Palace interior, taken by Benjamin Brecknell Turner (1815–94) in 1852. (The Museum acquired a positive of this image, as part of B.B. Turner's personal album, from his descendants in 1982). Gibbs-Smith contributed an introduction to

Gernsheim's book of the exhibition, published by Britain's leading art publishers, Phaidon Press.

The show drew many visitors, including Lady Clementina Tottenham. Perhaps she noticed a familiar-looking photograph of a young lady posed between balcony windows and a cheval glass. The label stated that it was by her grandmother's contemporary Oscar G. Rejlander. The photograph and attribution appeared as Plate 24 in the Phaidon book. The subject was titled *The Toilet*. (*The Toilette* might have sounded better.) However, the title should have been *Photographic Study,* or *Study from Life,* and the attribution to Lady Hawarden. The collection given by Lady Clementina Tottenham had been mislaid and forgotten during the turmoil of war and reorganization. Lady Clementina arrived to see the collection in 1952. 'Needless to say,' John Physick recalled in 1980, 'none of the photographs could be found. About a year later, Mr Gibbs-Smith moved a pile of boxes in the corner of his office. There in a mass of tight rolls were all the Hawarden photographs'.[3] Part of the Hawarden gift had been registered in 1947, but many of the photographs were not to be numbered until 1968. The Gernsheims re-attributed their print. Lady Hawarden's rediscovery did not really begin until the Library mounted a small display of her work in 1973. The painter Graham Ovenden published a selection of her works in a poorly printed but valuable book in 1975.

The success of *Masterpieces of Victorian Photography* spurred the Gernsheims to put forward an ambitious proposal. A letter to *The Times* was published under the heading 'NATIONAL COLLECTION OF PHOTOGRAPHY / FOSTERING APPRECIATION AND STUDY' on 3 March 1952. The Gernsheims drafted the letter with help from Nikolaus Pevsner, and approached Sir Leigh Ashton for his support. Ashton replied 'that while I am very much in sympathy with the project you put forward, I do not think that the Ministry of Education [the government department to which the V&A belonged] would wish me to sign such an appeal'.[4] He was, he added, barred in any case from making new commitments by the severe shortage of funds. Indeed, Ashton and James – heads of two of the country's major art institutions – haggled politely but firmly over who should pay the modest costs of painting the red walls of the installation for *Masterpieces of Victorian Photography*. This was still the age of austerity. In the end the letter was published over some distinguished signatures, including those of Clive Bell (art critic), Tom Hopkinson (editor of *Picture Post*), Nikolaus Pevsner (architectural historian *par excellence*), J.B. Priestley (writer and broadcaster) and J.R.H. Weaver (President of Trinity College, Oxford, whose platinum prints of Spanish historical architecture are well represented in the Photography Collection). The letter stated the problem: 'There is not a single museum or other public institution in Europe where the progress of photography can be studied – in spite of the indispensable part in our civilization played by photography'. It then offered a solution: 'Mr and Mrs Gernsheim are willing to present their collection to form the nucleus of such a public

59. ROGER MAYNE (British, born 1929). **Teds**, 1956. Gelatin-silver print. 10½ × 14⅝ in (26.7 × 37.2 cm). Bought from the photographer, 1964. 436–1964.

collection, provided suitable accommodation can be found, and a sufficient grant obtained to provide a centre'. The centre would preserve old photographs and encourage research, as well as fostering public appreciation of the art of photography by exhibiting leading contemporaries and acquiring examples of their work. It would do for photography what the newly established British Film Institute and National Film Library were doing for film. Following a correspondence on the subject in *The Times*, a second letter from the same signatories was published on 31 May 1952. It put forward more detailed plans: a permanent display, special exhibitions, a library, a photographic service providing copies for reproduction, lectures, publications including film strips with notes for schools and a specialist journal, and funds for acquisitions of old and modern photographs and books.

This admirable initiative fizzled out. There were understandable doubts at the V&A as to the role that the Gernsheims might play. They could surely not be expected to donate their collection without also donating themselves as directors of the new centre. At the Museum, however, these would have to be civil service appointments, by competition. Also, although times were certainly difficult financially, Ashton shared the disdain of his generation and class for photography as anything but a functional medium. He said so in distinct tones in exchanges with the photographer Roger Mayne in 1954 (Plate 59). Mayne was enthusiastically organizing exhibitions of international contemporary photography. As Press Secretary of the Combined Societies Association (CSA), a federation of photographic societies, Mayne wrote to Ashton to ask if the V&A would be interested in showing the CSA's exhibitions or buying from them. The response was clear:

> Dear Mayne,
> I am afraid it would only be a waste of time to come to discuss this question with me, as photographs are entirely outside the terms of reference of this museum. I could not, therefore, hold such an exhibition; nor could we take part in making a permanent collection of contemporary photographs.

When Mayne countered that the Gernsheim collection had been shown in 1951, Ashton replied (8 December 1954):

> I have nothing further to add to what I said before – but, if I must dot the 'i', photography is a purely mechanical process into which the artist does not enter. We exhibited Victorian photography in 1951 as part and parcel of the Centenary of 1851...[5]

The CSA exhibition for 1954–5 included works by leading British photographers such as Nigel Henderson, Mayne himself, Michael Peto, the young Frenchman Guy Bourdin (who became a sensation in fashion photography 20 years later) and the more seasoned masters Henri Cartier-Bresson, Willy Ronis, Werner Bischof and Robert

Capa. There were contributions from the Americans Paul Strand, Edward Weston and Minor White. Strand was now – during the McCarthy era in the United States – living in self-imposed exile in Paris, where Mayne visited him. Strand showed him original prints, carefully lighting each print with two lamps. He advised Mayne to improve his print quality. Mayne never forgot this lesson from the master, although he preferred a more urgent, grainy look for his own prints (Plate 59).

Mayne was a fierce public debater in the 1950s and made the essential point about the perennial photography/art theme. This is from an interview with Mayne by the modernist photographer Oswell Blakeston in 1956:

> He answers the question 'Is photography an art?' with 'No'. But then he would say neither is painting. 'All the "arts" are means of expression, which in the hands of artists can give works of art. Over a hundred years ago, D.O. Hill showed that photography can give works of art. That should be taken for granted nowadays; and yet every time there is a big camera exhibition, some critic starts the old cry – 'Is photography an art?'. It's just a silly way to frame the question.[6]

Most contemporary museum directors in Europe and the United States would have agreed with Sir Leigh Ashton. Sir Kenneth Clark, then Director of the National Gallery, insisted on the point. He lectured at the Royal Photographic Society on 13 October 1953 to commemorate the Society's centenary, speaking on 'The Relations of Photography and Painting'. He began by saying that it 'is the opinion held by many educated people that photography has nothing to do with art at all'. He summed up his entertaining if inaccurate lecture: 'The truth is that we do not turn to photography because it is a small and flat imitation of what we have seen, but because it deals with life'.

This was surely the essence of the problem in placing photography among the visual arts. In the middle of the twentieth century photography was, as it still is, the currency of thousands of social transactions. It had become as convenient, plentiful and flavourless as tap water. Photographs had become a necessary but unremarkable means of exchange, like stamps or coins. Such things might be fascinating for photographic experts, philatelists or numismatists but hardly for art connoisseurs or a general audience. Clark's treatment of the subject was distracted. The accomplished interpreter of the Old Masters in Trafalgar Square recoiled from the mediocrity of photography *en masse*. He had, he said, gone through thousands of press photographs when preparing his lecture. Understandably scornful of much Victorian photography, Clark was also out of sympathy with modernism: 'As an example, we may take a print by Moholy Nagy, the inventor of abstract photography, representing the famous Bauhaus; and personally I could not find a more economical combination of everything I dislike in art'.[7]

However, galleries had begun their job of selection. Henri Cartier-Bresson had his first show in Britain at another new institution, the Institute of Contemporary Arts (ICA), in 1952. The 1954–5 exhibition of the CSA was presented at the Whitechapel Art Gallery. Roger Mayne hung his dynamic London street photographs at the ICA in 1956. The ICA showed photography in many guises, notably through the exhibitions and other events organized by The Independent Group.[9] The ICA chairman, Sir Roland Penrose (husband of Lee Miller), was very keen to be involved with the London showing of Edward Steichen's sensational *The Family of Man*. However, the exhibition, first seen at The Museum of Modern Art, New York in 1955, was designed and promoted instead by *Picture Post* magazine and shown at the Royal Festival Hall (1956). (There is no evidence that this famous show was offered to the V&A and the Tate Gallery, as has sometimes been stated.) In 1957 Henri Cartier-Bresson held his second London show, this time at the Royal Society of British Artists Galleries. It was organized by Norman Hall, editor of the excellent magazine *Photography*, picture editor of *The Times*, and supporter and friend of Bill Brandt.

Helmut and Alison Gernsheim made another great contribution to photography's momentum by publishing the first edition of their monumental, if also maddening, *History of Photography* in 1955. (Factual errors are perhaps inevitable in such a large undertaking.) Helmut Gernsheim approached the V&A again in 1958. The Museum administered Osterley House, a National Trust property, in West London. Might Osterley's substantial top floor be available to house a 'National Collection of Photography'? The Museum's new director Sir Trenchard Cox and Charles Gibbs-Smith met Helmut Gernsheim on 17 November 1958. A familiar problem emerged. The Gernsheim collection would come with its owners, who would not be civil servants answerable to the Director of the Museum. A testy exchange of letters between Gernsheim and Gibbs-Smith occurred in 1964. Initially about copyright in Paul Martin photographs, it broadened out to address the Museum's overall view of photography. It concluded with a prophetic paragraph, dated 28 June 1964, from Gernsheim:

> I feel sure that in another decade, if not sooner, the V&A will follow other art museums and museums of applied art in having an *active* photographic department in which creative photography and historic photographs from its origins to today, will be collected and exhibited, as we suggested thirteen years ago. If not yourself, it will be the lot of some future public relations officer to defend the Museum extension as hotly as your present and previous Directors have claimed it to be outside the scope of the Museum activities. Perhaps the first sign of coming new trends is already implied in the Museum's recent purchase of some contemporary photographs, of which I have just heard.[8]

The Gernsheim Collection was sold to the Harry Ransom Humanities Research Center, University of Texas at Austin, in 1964.

Photography, denied access at the front door of the V&A, flew in through a back window. Having no place in the Art Library, contemporary creative photography acquisitions began to be made instead by the Circulation Department. Circulation, the travelling exhibitions' department, has featured earlier in the story, touring Cameron's photographs in the 1860s. In the 1960s, it provided shows to some 180 museums and galleries throughout the United Kingdom. Exhibitions and smaller loan collections travelled to about 230 art schools, technical colleges, colleges of education, universities and so on. The Circulation Department spearheaded the scholarly study of Victorian and Edwardian Decorative Art, hitherto generally despised subjects, in an exhibition of that title held in 1952. A startling fact must be remembered. Until 1966 the V&A's Primary galleries included only objects made before 1830. So did much – if by no means all – of the Museum's expertise. Circulation Department staff pioneered more recent periods on behalf of the Museum in general. In 1962 Circulation organized *London 1862*, which commemorated the International Exhibition of 1862. The exhibition included a satellite display, which dealt with the 1862 Exhibition buildings, showing documents, prints and a striking selection from the Photography Collection's rich holdings. It was organized by Betty Bradford of the Circulation Department, who wrote it up for *The Architectural Review* (July 1962). Two years later Circulation toured *Masterpieces of Victorian Photography*, composed of modern copy prints from originals in the Photography Collection and the Royal Photographic Society.

60. IDA KAR (British, born Armenia, 1908–74). **Gino Severini in his Studio**, *c.*1955. Gelatin-silver print. 24 × 30 in (61 × 76 cm). Bought from the photographer, 1964. Circ.416–1964.

In 1964 Carol Hogben of the Circulation Department began to acquire contemporary photographs for touring, particularly to colleges. He started by buying works by Ida Kar (Plate 60) and Roger Mayne. For the first time in about a century, the Museum had a member of staff who frequented photography exhibitions with a view to buying. And for the first time since the turn of the century there were important photography exhibitions from which to buy.

The 'Sixties was the crucial time of change for photography in Britain and the United States. There was a quantum leap in interest and activity. As we have seen, there had always been photographers, critics and collectors who believed passionately in the art of photography. Why, however, should their cause have been vindicated, with growing completeness, from the 1960s? In Britain there was a large expansion in numbers attending university and therefore, arguably, a broader social range of museum visitors. Photography also became part of art's mainstream through the silkscreen printing revolution (much collected by Circulation) and as a favoured means of documentation by Conceptualist artists. These occurrences may have contributed to the sudden and widespread re-classification of photography, but surely do not fully explain it.

According to figures kindly supplied by the National Museum of Photography, Film and Television, Britain had 3.2 million television license holders in 1952. There

61. Bill Brandt (British, 1904–83). **Nude**, 1956. Gelatin-silver print. 17½ × 14¾ in (44.5 × 37.5 cm). Bought from the photographer, 1965. Circ.26–1965.

was a marked increase at the time of the Coronation of Elizabeth II in 1953, but the most dramatic leap in access to television occurred in the eight to ten years after 1954. By 1959 over half the homes in the nation had access to a set. It is perhaps more than a coincidence that photography became an art worth exhibiting and collecting once more at the end of this ten-year period. When television assumed the dominant role in news and mass-information, photography again became visible, exhibitable and collectable.

Carol Hogben was about the same age as Mayne, whose work he knew through the ICA show of 1956 and his vigorous presence in the British print media. In 1960 the Whitechapel Art Gallery – which had become, under Bryan Robertson, London's most important avant-garde gallery – staged a spectacular retrospective by Ida Kar. In emulation of *The Family of Man*, the prints were on a grand scale. They were, incidentally, produced by the Autotype Co., which had printed photographs (in the permanent carbon process) for Julia Margaret Cameron.[10] With 10,000 visitors, 35 reviews and some sales at prices between £50 and £100, Kar's show was a milestone event in the repositioning of photography. It duly impressed Carol Hogben. Although the costs of printing her exhibition had proved crippling, Kar very generously offered the Museum her own selection of her portraits – 18 large prints for the reduced price of £100. Her choice included the poised and memorable *Gino Severini in his Studio* from the mid-1950s (Plate 60).

Hogben was also greatly impressed by a travelling exhibition of Edward Steichen's photographs organized by the United States Information Service – important promoters of photography in these years – which was shown at the American Embassy in London in 1965. Two years later twelve newly printed Steichens were bought at $100 apiece, perhaps reflecting the more developed market for photography – already – in the States. The photographer donated two dye-transfer prints after his early colour photographs in the Autochrome process.

Growing up in the 1940s, Hogben had been aware of Bill Brandt's photographs in the magazines *Picture Post* and *Lilliput*. Brandt's reputation was dramatically renewed and extended with the publication of *Perspective of Nudes* in 1961. At the end of the war, Brandt had bought a second-hand camera which promised him an imaginative, even Surreal, alternative to the Rolleiflex he had used for his landmark work as a photojournalist. It was a Kodak camera with a wide-angle lens, as employed by auctioneers and the police to make photographic inventories of rooms. Brandt learned how to use it to create an extraordinary set of variations on the female nude (Plate 61). Perhaps he drew inspiration for the series from the Picasso-Matisse show of 1945? Hogben bought 26 prints from *Perspective of Nudes* for £5 each in 1965. Despite Brandt's fame, his revolutionary book was far from being universally admired or commercially successful at the time of its first publication. The nominal price of the prints may have reflected Brandt's pleasure in the Museum's interest in his work and

Dr Pepper
FROSTY COLD
Dr Pepper

62. Henri Cartier-Bresson (French, born 1908).
Mississippi, 1961.
Gelatin-silver print.
9½ × 14⅛ in (24.2 × 36 cm). Bought from the photographer, 1978. 682–1978.

its presentation to a nationwide student audience. However, although Brandt had sold some prints to The Museum of Modern Art and George Eastman House (in Rochester, NY) these were very special institutions. Although some museums, and a rare collector like Helmut Gernsheim might buy, there was still no market for photography as prints.

There was, however, a new audience for photographic exhibitions. The colleges ordered more and more of the sets of photographs that Hogben acquired. The Circulation Department was unlike the curatorial departments of the Museum not only in its outward-looking and modernist stance; even though it covered an enormous subject-range, it was also relatively well funded. In addition, revenues from colleges and museums for loan exhibitions and smaller collections were spent on new acquisitions for touring. A programme of purchasing and lending photographs was therefore pushed ahead. These acquisitions were usually of fifteen prints, although sometimes more. The department's needs coincided with the availability of a new range of portfolios. These were published mainly in New York by such companies as Parasol Press and Witkin-Berley, and occasionally by photographers themselves.

Acquisitions included: Cecil Beaton's multi-exposure photographs, 1965; Man Ray's limited edition of 20 Rayographs, published in Stuttgart in 1963; Herbert Bayer's photomontages from 1929–36 (including Plate 55), 1969; Don McCullin's gift of 17 prints from his exhibition *The Destruction Business* at the ICA, 1969; Jacques-Henri Lartigue's portfolio of new prints from his classic early negatives, 1971; Gerry Cranham's sports photographs, 1971; David Hockney's personal photographs, 1971; Berenice Abbott's portfolio of her gelatin-silver prints from Atget's negatives, 1974; Diane Arbus's only portfolio, *A Box of Ten Photographs*, bought in 1974; Ansel Adams's *Portfolio V*, 1974. Young documentary photographers whose work was acquired at this time included Nick Hedges of the campaigning group Shelter, the black American Sylvester Jacobs, Cristobal Melian from Spain and – then a stateless person in exile from Czechoslovakia – Josef Koudelka. Fifteen works from Koudelka's *Gypsies* series were bought in 1976. A career selection was acquired from Britain's Raymond Moore in the same year. Photographs were also acquired from fine artists like the Los Angeles installation artist Larry Bell, and from Barry Flanagan and John Stezaker; and from conceptual artists such as John Blake, Roelof Louw, John Hilliard, and Bernd and Hilla Becher.

The Circulation Department also presented full-scale exhibitions, first at the V&A and then on tour. These were curated by Carol Hogben and his assistants Elizabeth Bailey and (from 1970) the present writer. The modernist/populist streak of the department is reflected in the shows: *Henri Cartier–Bresson*, 1969; *Gerry Cranham Sports Photographs*, 1971; *The Compassionate Camera: Dustbowl Pictures* (photographs from the files of the Farm Security Administration in the Library of Congress), 1973; *Jazz Seen: The Face of Black Music. Photographs by Valerie Wilmer*, 1973; *Hollywood Still*

63. Gerry Cranham (British, born 1929). **Spurs Goalkeeper John Hollowbread Leaps into the Air as his Team Scores at Tottenham**, 1964. Gelatin-silver print. 15 × 19¾ in (38.5 × 50.2 cm). Bought from the photographer, 1971. E.1081–1996.

Photography 1927–41 from the John Kobal Collection, 1974; *The Land: 20th Century Landscape Photographs Selected by Bill Brandt*, 1975; *Ansel Adams Photographs*, 1976.

Bill Brandt's exhibition *The Land* opened with a white room containing one almost completely white photograph. The photograph had been taken over Antarctica from a United States Navy weather research plane.[11] The show ended with a NASA photograph of a crescent earth seen from the moon. In between were many of the most extraordinary – and now very well known – landscape photographs made in the twentieth century, beginning with Steichen's early landscapes (lent from the Alfred Stieglitz Collection at the Metropolitan Museum of Art, New York). Each work was separately spot-lit. The Museum acquired everything from the show that was available, including works by Ansel Adams, Paul Strand, Edward Weston (and his sons Brett and Cole), plus post-war talents such as Morley Baer, Wynn Bullock, Harry Callahan, Paul Caponigro, Pirkle Jones, Eliot Porter, Aaron Siskind, Minor White and Paul Caponigro. Other purchases were made from Australia's Grant Mudford, Japan's Hiroshi Hamaya, New Zealand's Brian Brake, and Europeans like Brandt himself, Brassai, Cartier-Bresson, Robert Doisneau, Mario Giacomelli, Fay Godwin, Don McCullin, George Rodger and others. Of the six Paul Strand landscapes, two were given by the photographer and four by the Gordon Fraser Charitable Trust through the National Art Collections Fund (NACF). The selection represented Strand landscapes from Nova Scotia, New Mexico, France, Morocco and the Outer Hebrides. They were the first photographs to be donated to a museum through the NACF, which has generously made possible many subsequent major photographic purchases by museums in Britain. A set of *Equivalents* by Alfred Stieglitz was borrowed for *The Land* from the Art Institute of Chicago. Seven *Equivalents* were bought in the 1980s.

Ansel Adams attended the opening of his exhibition of 100 photographs in 1976. The show toured to Moscow, Rome and Paris. Polaroid Corporation supported the show financially and, at Adams's request, the gallery walls were painted a desert terracotta colour of exactly 18½ per cent reflectance. Bill Brandt and Brassai came to the opening and were photographed by Paul Joyce and Richard Sadler sitting with Adams in the Museum's garden. He had already sold twelve of his most famous photographs to the Museum, for *The Land*, at the nominal sum of one thousand pounds. Now he donated 20 more prints. The Ansel Adams holding of 40 photographs is among the most popular with visitors to the Print Room. A memorial exhibition was held to commemorate his death in 1984.

Of all these activities, the most important was the Cartier-Bresson retrospective (1969). Over the next nine years it toured to over 100 centres throughout the country in various forms and played a major part in changing the climate of opinion about photography in Britain. Whereas the 1957 Cartier-Bresson exhibition, designed by Alan Irvine, had been shown as large prints mounted on screens, Hogben framed

64. Don McCullin (British, born 1935). **Rhodesian Mercenary, Stanleyville, Congo**, 1967. Gelatin-silver print. 28 × 18 in (71 × 45.5 cm). Given by the photographer, *c.*1969. E.1082– 1996.

the prints – but in unusual ways. Some prints 'floated' inside frames, protected by perspex (plexiglass) but with no over-mat. Other photographs were mounted on to boards with raised sides (but without perspex). The idea was to provide some physical presence and protection for the prints, while avoiding the conventions used for older graphic material. The exhibition was presented at the V&A with slide projections, white walls, a table of the master's publications, and white Arne Jacobsen 'Tulip' chairs. The chair-seats were very grey by the time this sensationally popular show closed.

This was the V&A's first serious showing of contemporary photographs, as an art medium in their own right, since that of Julia Margaret Cameron's in 1865. Carol Hogben wrote an eloquent catalogue essay which presented Cartier-Bresson in a particular way:

> Putting photographs in frames, and showing them on walls where paintings would more usually be hung, involves a certain risk of mistaking the medium. The primary existence of a painting is clearly in the unique physical object, fashioned by the artist himself. Any reproductive illustration of its image is merely some entirely secondary reference. It is the situation of most professional photographers today, however, that the *primary* existence of their work lies in its printed reproduction, whether in the pages of a book or in the so-called glossy magazines. The once-off enlargement, placed in a gallery exhibition, is in most cases a by-product of their work.[12]

Cartier-Bresson was presented very much as a photojournalist. Hogben pursued interesting analogies between photography and writing:

> It is precisely one of the things that distinguishes a practitioner of his rank that from looking at a body of his work one is able, without any difficulty at all, to apprehend the broad qualities of his mind – in this case, his compassion, his hatred of pretence, his sense of irony, his care of innocence. It is a mind far nearer to Turgenev, shall we say, than to a Toulouse-Lautrec.

Cartier-Bresson was shown in 1969 as a great contemporary rather than as a modern master. The show was weighted towards the last ten years of his work – as represented in Plate 62. Addressing the time-honoured difficulties of placing photography as a medium, Hogben suggested

> that it may be more helpful to be thinking of photography as closer to writing than to graphic art. For the materials that a writer uses are common to everyone. Every one of us strings sentences together from morning to night, but nobody gets in a trauma as to how one can possibly be expected to tell who is a fine professional writer and who is none.

Jazzette

65. Val Wilmer (British, born 1941). **Kenneth Terroade in a Flat in Putney, London**, July 1971. Gelatin-silver print. 19½ × 13½ in (49.5 × 34.5 cm). Bought from the photographer, 1973. Circ.235–1973.

Hogben himself could write splendidly, as suggested by the first sentence in a potentially awkward letter to Bill Brandt on 8 October 1965: 'You will, I hope, be flattered to hear that two of your nude photographs were stolen from the first college to which they were sent on loan!' Brandt was not perturbed by this and made two replacement prints. When he heard that the stolen prints had been recovered, Brandt wrote: 'I had just made new ones for you – they look very nice & are ready for you if a thief happens to fancy these particular pictures again. But in the meantime I am not charging for them'.[13]

Things began to move more quickly. In 1968 the Welsh Arts Council showed a photographer for the first time – Raymond Moore. Roy Strong, dashing young Director of the National Portrait Gallery, staged (definitely the *mot juste*) *Beaton Portraits* in 1968. The ICA showed *Spectrum: The Diversity of Photography* in 1969, featuring Dorothy Bohm, Don McCullin, Enzo Ragazzini and Tony Ray-Jones. The Arts Council of Great Britain presented its first retrospective exhibition by a photographer in 1970 – Bill Brandt. The show was selected by John Szarkowski and came on tour from The Museum of Modern Art, New York. (It afterwards toured the UK.) The Photographers' Gallery was founded by Sue Davies and Dorothy Bohm in 1971. The Arts Council of Great Britain organized *'From Today Painting is Dead': The Beginnings of Photography* at the V&A in 1972. This theatrically presented exhibition, designed by Robin Wade, included many important prints from the V&A collection, such as the Watson *Nude*, a group of Hawardens, Silvy's *River Scene, France* and many other intriguing items. It was selected by Dr David Thomas of the Science Museum and organized by Joanna Drew of the Arts Council. Dr Thomas also showed a group of Daguerreotypes, then owned by Leonard Russell, and brilliantly attributed them to De Ste Croix (Plate 3). The show gave considerable impetus to the general appreciation of early photography. However, it was one of the last important museum exhibitions in which original photographs and copy prints were displayed side by side.

The Photography Collection in the National Art Library was becoming more active and better known. Peter Castle, the librarian responsible for it, presented photographic displays in the Library's galleries, including Lady Hawarden, Roger Fenton and Agnes B. Warburg in 1972–3. He published *Collecting and Valuing Old Photographs* in 1973.

In 1972 another photographic controversy stirred the correspondence columns of *The Times*. This one concerned the proposed sale by the Royal Academy of the Hill and Adamson albums that had long been in its library. In the excitement about the potential loss of 'heritage' items to overseas buyers, it was forgotten by many that the V&A owned a total of 162 Hill and Adamson calotypes, including two fine albums given in 1868 (Plate 7). The National Portrait Gallery under Dr Roy Strong was keen to acquire the Academy's volumes. The V&A's Director, Sir John Pope-Hennessy, took a different view. He regarded the Hill and Adamsons at the V&A, together with

Offenes Feuer
— Rauchen —
im Bereich der
Gaskugeln
verboten

66. BERNHARD and HILLA BECHER (German, born 1931 and 1934). **Gas Holder, Power Station, Essen-Karhap, Ruhr District**. Gelatin-silver print, 1973. 15⅝ × 11⅞ in (39.8 × 30.2 cm). Bought 1975. Circ.642–1975.

the thousands of prints and negatives at the Scottish National Portrait Gallery, as a sufficient national holding. In a letter to C.W. Wright of the Department of Education and Science on 13 December 1972, Sir John wrote this significant sentence: 'It is, of course, this Museum, not the National Portrait Gallery, which houses the principal collection of historic photographs; the distinction between the two areas of interest is essentially that the Portrait Gallery is concerned only with photographs as portraiture, while we in this Museum are concerned with photographs as art'.[14] A brief typescript from about the same date, titled *Early Photographs in the Victoria and Albert Museum Library*, describes the collection. There is a hand-written addition: 'In lieu of a "stated" National Collection of Early Photographs, we are that collection in fact'. On 4 June 1973 Pope-Hennessy wrote a minute on the subject of 'Photographic Collections':

> 1. I have felt for some time that the arrangement whereby our photographic collection is cared for by the Library is illogical and should be reviewed. My reasons are as follows.
>
> 2. The collection owes its distinction to its rich holdings of early photographs. These are now well catalogued and, on a minimal basis, well exhibited. The future of the collection cannot, however, be conceived simply in passive terms, since there is a tendency at the present time (i) to accept that photographs are, or are susceptible of being, works of art, and (ii) to recognise that photographs by artists have a direct relevance both to the personality of the artist and to his work in other forms.[15]

In category one Pope-Hennessy placed the work of Cartier-Bresson and the FSA photographers (Dorothea Lange, Walker Evans *et al.*). He placed in the second category photographs by Larry Bell, which relate intimately to his glass installations. Pope-Hennessy cited the American museum practice of establishing either a separate Department of Photography or a section in a larger department dealing with graphic art. He proposed the latter solution. But this could happen – given the Museum's jigsaw puzzle of space – only when the theatre collection left Prints and Drawings to become the V&A's Theatre Museum in its own Central London home. However, before then, Sir John himself had moved to Bloomsbury (in 1973), as Director of the British Museum.

Carol Hogben had written in his Cartier-Bresson essay that 'at least in one literal sense, it could be claimed of photography that it is the most strictly popular of all arts. Millions practise it for themselves. Everybody, confronted with a photograph, feels he knows what he is looking at and what the subject is supposed to be. The sensation of recognition can be infinitely savoured, with enduring pleasure'. Hogben was responsible for acquiring the brave and unforgettable images by the young photojournalist Don McCullin (Plate 64). Hogben himself directed the exhibition of the outstanding sports photographer Gerry Cranham, who contrived to express much of the magic of 'the people's game' in one image (Plate 63). Hogben was also happy for his juniors to develop their own shows. Elizabeth Bailey curated *Jazz Seen: The Face of Black Music* by Val Wilmer, who was then still in the early years of her distinguished career (Plate 65). The exhibition, which was accompanied by a series of jazz concerts in the V&A garden, helped to launch Val Wilmer into the male-dominated arena of British photojournalism. (The Association of Fashion, Advertising and Editorial Photographers was founded in London in 1971: of the 400 members just four were women.) She had always wanted to do more than the obvious, commercial 'blowing' shot, to show 'who the musician is when he/she is not actually involved in creativity or in earning a living'. With a selfconsciousness new to the time, she described herself as a 'creative photographer' and devoted herself to the photography of jazz as a self-imposed, long-term assignment.[16]

Already artists from fine art backgrounds had begun to make photographs. In Düsseldorf, the partnership of Bernhard and Hilla Becher began a lifetime of work concentrated on the idea of 'Anonymous Sculpture'. Their carefully photographed, minimally inflected documents selected and presented functional structures as a kind of anonymous, collective sculpture (Plate 66). Although the notion of 'The Functional Tradition' in architecture was popular with critics in the 1950s and 1960s, and inspired wonderful photographs by Eric de Maré (well represented in the collection), that movement had passed by the gasometers and coalwashing plants sought out internationally by the Bechers. A new generation of artists using photographs and text came to prominence in Britain with the exhibition *The New Art* at the Hayward Gallery in 1972. Artists of this new generation were also acquired by Circulation. John Hilliard elegantly demonstrated the arbitrariness and artificiality of camera positions and colour materials. Hamish Fulton, trained as a sculptor, revolutionized the idea of sculpture as movement through landscape and time using camera and text (Plate 67). The Circulation programme was hospitable to many kinds of photography, finding them all 'susceptible of being works of art'. However, the Circulation Department was closed, just as a new life opened for the Photography Collection.

67. Hamish Fulton (British, born 1945). **Five Knots for Five Days of Walking.** Gelatin-silver print, text and frame. 45⅛ × 33³⁄₁₆ in (114.6 × 84.4 cm). Bought 1976. Circ.362–1976.

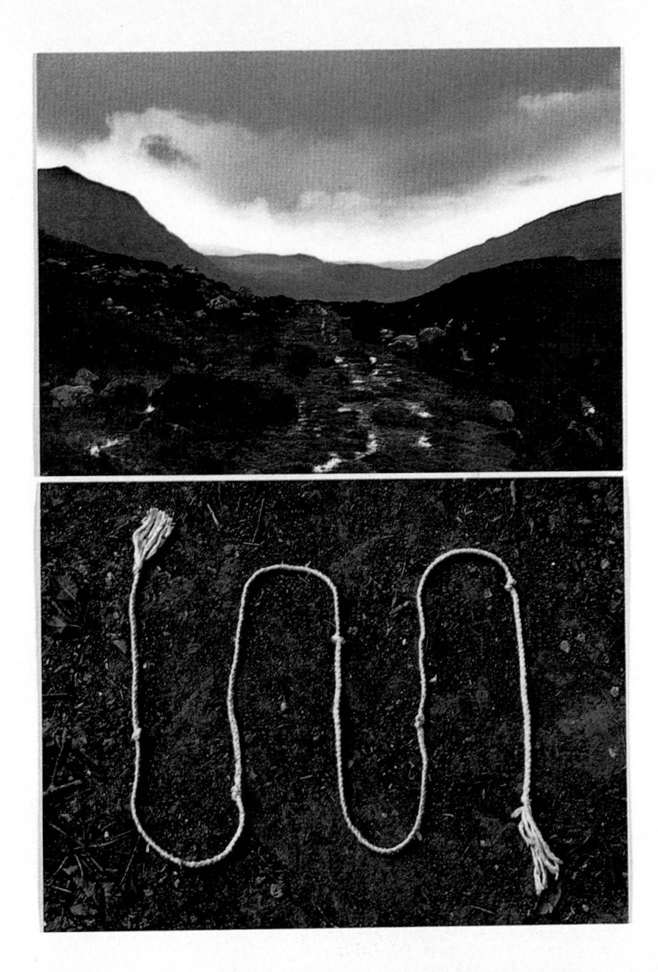

FIVE KNOTS FOR FIVE DAYS OF WALKING

THE STRING WAS BRAIDED AND KNOTTED AT BOTH ENDS
AND ONE KNOT TIED AFTER EACH DAY

ISLE OF LEWIS & HARRIS
SCOTLAND
SUMMER
1973

CHAPTER SEVEN

The National Collection of the Art of Photography

In 1950 a professional photograph was typically a 10 × 8 in (25 × 20 cm) black and white print that was passed to a designer and then a printer to appear in a magazine. It was then discarded, filed or forgotten. In 1980 a professional photograph might also be a handsome work of graphic art, generally twice the size of its predecessor. It might be made by hand, in one of a variety of craft processes, expressly for exhibition in and preservation by museums. It was usually made to last: printing was to archival standards. Quite frequently it was issued in a signed and strictly limited edition. This transformation is perfectly demonstrated in the work and career of Irving Penn. *The Harlequin Dress (Lisa Fonssagrives–Penn), New York*, 1950, printed in platinum and palladium metals in 1979 (Plate 68), was bought by the V&A in 1981. 1950 was Irving Penn's miraculous year, when his *Black and White Vogue Cover* illustrated all international editions of the magazine. He photographed the Autumn Collections for the first time – and for eternity – in a north-light Paris studio. He captured many of his *petits métiers* series, as well as classic portraits and nudes. In the same year Penn and Lisa Fonssagrives married in London.

The Harlequin Dress is a collaboration between photographer and model. The tile-sized checks of the afternoon dress are set off by the mask-like face, black hat and gloves, black-dyed mink lei and mock pearls. The cigarette and flicked up eye make-up add a certain smoulder to the atmosphere. The dress has the characteristic features of 'The New Look', the soft shoulder-line, voluminous skirt and – invisible but inevitable – nipped-in waist. Despite appearances, the dress was not *haute couture*. By Jerry Parnis, who designed moderately priced clothes, it retailed for $25 at a time when *Vogue* cost 35 cents. The 'ribbing' of the cloth, a rayon or cotton piqué, is subtly caught in the superb print. Penn fell into his 'platinum obsession' when commercially made gelatin-silver paper fell short of what it had been in earlier years. There is astonishing texture in the blacks and whites, as well as warmth and depth. The prints were made by contact, usually from enlarged negatives, on hand-coated paper. Exposures ran from minutes to two hours or more. Some of the prints, like this one, were made in two coatings, each of different combinations of platinum and palladium (and sometimes iridium). In such cases there are usually two or more negatives of varying contrasts used in making a single print. This work was part of a group acquired by purchase and gift from Penn's exhibition at Marlborough Fine Art in London in 1981. *Irving Penn*, a retrospective exhibition from The Museum of Modern Art, New York, was shown at the V&A in 1987. It was one of the V&A's

68. Irving Penn (American, born 1917). **The Harlequin Dress (Lisa Fonssagrives-Penn), New York**, 1950. Platinum and palladium print. 21½ × 19 in (54.6 × 48.3 cm). Bought 1981. Ph.397–1981.

most successful ever exhibitions. The acquisitions from Penn, and the presentation of his retrospective exhibition, came about because the V&A had a new Director who was passionate about photography.

Henry Cole was 44 when he took charge of the Department of Practical Art in 1852. He grew up with photography, was well positioned to observe its experimental years, and began to use it as soon as the medium matured and the moment materialized in 1851. Roy Strong became Director of the V&A in 1974 at the age of 38. He too grew up with photography – in the form of illustrated art books and topical magazines. As adept with publicity as Cole, photographed by Beaton and other notables, Strong was the first British museum director since Cole to understand and love photography. Whereas Cole championed photography as the great popularizing instrument of his time, Strong promoted it as one of the great popular arts.

When Strong came to the V&A he had impressive qualifications as scholar, administrator and modernizer. He had already demonstrated his leadership in the photographic field. Britain's first museum show of a living photographer was the 1968 National Portrait Gallery retrospective exhibition *Beaton Portraits* by Sir Cecil Beaton (1904–81). Strong asked the ballet designer Richard Buckle to stage it. The show was flamboyant and theatrical, with a different selection of music playing in each room. Strong went on to set up a Department of Film and Photography at the National Portrait Gallery, with Colin Ford as its Keeper, in 1972. He chaired the Arts Council of Great Britain's newly formed Photography Committee. The Arts Council appointed a Photography Officer, Barry Lane, in 1971 and, among many initiatives, organized *'From Today Painting is Dead'* at the V&A in 1972 and *The Real Thing: An Anthology of British Photographs, 1840–1950*, selected by Ian Jeffrey, at the Hayward Gallery in 1974.

Photography was among Strong's priorities when he became Director of the V&A. Like Pope-Hennessy before him, he had to wait for certain pieces to fall into place before undertaking a large-scale reorganization. However, he quickly began to initiate major photographic acquisitions. In 1976 the Library bought key works from *Photography: The First 80 Years* at Colnaghi's, Britain's first major commercial show of early photographs. Purchases included *Don Quixote in his Study* by Lake Price (Figure 3), Steichen's *Portrait of Anatole France* (Plate 46), Kühn's *Portrait of Alfred Stieglitz* (Plate 47) and *The Steerage* (printed in photogravure on vellum) by Stieglitz himself. The Library also bought representative groups of prints by classic British moderns, such as the *Picture Post* veterans Bert Hardy and Godfrey Thurston Hopkins, George Rodger, co-founder of Magnum, and the young star Tony Ray-Jones. Through the Circulation Department, meanwhile, the Museum was buying 200 photographs by Bill Brandt.

Larger events intervened. Britain's serious economic troubles in 1976 prompted drastic action: Civil Service departments were ordered to cut their staff by 11 per cent. The result at the V&A was the closure of the Circulation Department. This was and has remained a controversial decision. However, many Circulation staff, as well as the Circulation collections, were integrated into the institution's curatorial departments, thus furthering Strong's plan to bring the Museum's expertise and collections up to date. In 1977 the responsibility for the Photography Collection was formally transferred from the National Art Library to the Department of Prints and Drawings, where it was joined by all the photographs acquired by Circulation. The Office of Arts and Libraries designated the V&A as the national collection of the art of photography in the UK's system of national museums. Interviews were held and the present writer was appointed Curator. Gernsheim had prophesied correctly, except that the V&A public relations department had no problems announcing the new dispensation. Photography had become a familiar, and highly successful, part of the V&A's exhibition programme.

When the Department of Prints, Drawings & Photographs and Paintings was established in 1977 (later simplified to Prints, Drawings and Paintings), Strong committed himself to a ten-year programme of major photographic acquisitions. He sensed, correctly, that this was the last time when significant acquisitions of the rarest material could be made. Many of the photographs in this book have, as the captions show, museum numbers from 1977 to 1987 and were acquired during that important phase. Strong's aim was to build on the superb existing holdings and to establish a national photographic collection worthy of the art. Although the Photography Collection and its staff did not physically join the other graphic collections until the Henry Cole Wing was renovated in the early 1980s, from 1977 Museum visitors were shown photographs in the Print Room rather than the National Art Library. The vast archive of nineteenth-century photographs of paintings was moved from the basement or 'Crypt' of the Museum, where dust blew in from Cromwell Road, and placed on loan at the University of Essex, where it was used in teaching art history. The Photography Collection began to be catalogued in detail, along the lines of Prints and Drawings.

Strong was eager to acquire major works in the fast-moving photographic market of the late 1970s and 1980s. Sotheby's had pioneered photographic sales, from 1971, and Christie's and Phillips soon followed. One of the most impressive of all British photographs appeared at auction at Christie's South Kensington in 1978. It was the finest piece in one of the most spectacular photographic albums ever sold.[1] The so-called 'grey albums', sold by Christie's from 1978 to 1981, contained hundreds of known and previously unknown photographs by Roger Fenton. *Nubian Model Reclining*, a salted paper print, was lot 279 in a sale of nineteenth and twentieth-century photographs held on 27 June 1978.[1] The Christie's estimate was £2,000. Strong authorized a bid of £2,000, and then – on the day of the sale – doubled it. In the event the Museum was underbidder. The successful bid of £5,400 was made by Sean

Thackrey, of the San Francisco gallery Thackrey and Robertson. He was the adviser and representative of William Rubel, a Californian publisher who became one of the major photography collectors of the time. With buyer's premium, the lot price was £6,480. Application was made to the Department of Trade for a license to export the photograph. Britain's leading photographic historians, including the doyen of photographic studies in Britain, Professor Aaron Scharf, argued that the Fenton – of which no other print is known – was too important to be allowed to leave the country. The Export Licensing Committee decided, however, to grant the license. Soon afterwards the chairman of the committee, the Renaissance historian Professor John White, asked Aaron Scharf for lunch to talk about photography. He received a dusty answer.[2] Scharf himself had been born and raised in the United States and had no doubt benefited from America's more discriminating and positive view of the medium. A book that highlights the difference between America and Europe in this regard is *Art and Life in America* (1949, third printing 1956) by Oliver W. Larkins. The plates include works by major American photographers. Edward Hopper's *The City* unpatronizingly faces *Two-Family Houses, Bethlehem, Pa.* by Walker Evans. Larkins discusses recent American photographers like Weegee, Barbara Morgan and Lisette Model. Fine photographs were accepted in America alongside the other visual arts. This was not the case in Britain or other European countries. The Fenton is now among the most highly valued photographs in the world. It returned to Britain to distinguish the exhibition *Roger Fenton – Photographer*, shown at the Hayward Gallery in 1988, but it is very unlikely to return on a permanent basis. However, thanks to the forebearance and generosity of another major collector, Paul Walter of New York City, the Museum was able to acquire – from the same 'grey albums' – another salted paper print of the same (European) model. Fenton's only semi-nude figure was bought in 1979.

The Museum was more fortunate, and more determined, at auction in 1979 when a particularly important group of works by Robert Howlett came to auction. The famous portrait of Isambard Kingdom Brunel and the reportage of the *Great Eastern* under construction had been exhibited at the South Kensington Museum in 1858, as we saw in chapter two (Plates 21–22). Now, at last, the Museum bought the portrait – setting a new world record price of £7,600 – plus fourteen views of the ship and its builders. From the same sale came Roger Fenton's personal album of Crimean views – including the image of his 'Photographic Van' (Figure 5) – which he had presented to his daughter. The album has now been fully conserved so that the photographs are preserved in the original sequence, while also being conveniently removable for exhibitions.[3]

The V&A collecting policy gained much from the pioneering work of the Department of Photography founded in 1940 at The Museum of Modern Art, New York. The Photography Gallery at MoMA has been an inspiration to generations of visitors. The department's publications have also been widely and deservedly influential. Photography's aesthetics and history have been eloquently discussed by John Szarkowski in a career of many books and exhibitions. The present writer has visited MoMA regularly since 1970. A conversation with John Szarkowski in the mid-'Seventies led to the rediscovery of the V&A's Atget collection, which was exhibited for the first time at the Salford Art Gallery in 1980. Like MoMA, the V&A embraces the best of both 'functional' and 'fine art' photography. The creative interaction between the fine art and functional photographic traditions was the subject of *American Photography 1890–1965*, directed by Szarkowski's successor Peter Galassi. It was shown at the V&A to acclaim in the winter of 1996–7. The formulations of Roger Mayne and Carol Hogben quoted in the last chapter are obviously relevant to the V&A's approach. Photography is collected as a visual language and 'an independent art'. It is world-wide in scope and places a strong emphasis on the contemporary.

It is not, of course, the only national collection of photographs.The V&A is part of a network of eleven national collections of photography in the UK. The Committee of National Collections was formed in 1987 and includes: Birmingham Central Library, the British Film Institute, the Imperial War Museum, the National Buildings Record, the National Library of Wales, the National Museum of Photography, Film and Television, the National Portrait Gallery, the Public Record Office, the Royal Photographic Society, the Scottish National Portrait Gallery and the V&A. There are many other photography collections of national importance, such as the Royal Archives, Windsor Castle. The British Library appointed a curator of photographs in 1996. In addition, there are major collections of contemporary photography at the British Council, the South Bank Centre and the Tate Gallery, plus important holdings at the Harris Museum and Art Gallery, Preston, Leeds City Art Gallery and Southampton City Art Gallery.

Part of the practical aim of the V&A's collecting policy is to acquire high-quality material for rotating displays in its own permanent photography gallery: to apply to photography the kind of systematic presentation referred to by Dr Waagen in the opening pages of this book. Another aim is to acquire in depth, to serve the needs of museums, galleries and independent exhibition organizers across the United Kingdom. Many kinds of show can be drawn out of the collection, such as the large exhibition of *Street Photography* shown in 1994–5. In 1996 photographs were lent to exhibitions on themes as various as *The Desert* and *Kiss This*. Photographs are also lent to venues worldwide. *The Golden Age of British Photography, 1839–1900*, was produced in 1984 in collaboration with the Philadelphia Museum of Art and toured to five United States cities in 1984–5. The exhibition was given permanent form in a catalogue, printed to the highest standard by Meriden Gravure. The lively state of British photography in the 1980s – plus its expanding ambitions, larger prints and new media such as holography – was recognized in a two-part exhibition, *Towards a Bigger Picture*

(1987–8). The complete show was presented at the Tate Gallery, Liverpool in 1989. Aperture, New York, published a book of the same title, which reflects the contents of the show, in 1988.

Sometimes one photograph may capture an epoch and an artist. Sometimes, for a major career, a wider range of work has been acquired. Sometimes, too, a photographic 'work' is a carefully constructed series, sequence or ensemble. Certain relatively large groups of photographs are discussed in the rest of this chapter.

Photographs by Beaton were bought by the Circulation Department and shown in the touring exhibition *Modern Photography* (1967). These were mainly his multiple-exposure portraits of artists, dancers, poets and other celebrities. Beaton sold his personal archive of prints and negatives to Sotheby's in 1977. A series of Beaton sales took place, at which the Photography Collection acquired a broader representation of Beaton's work. His 1967 portrait of the model Twiggy, walking (almost) on air in his South Kensington house, perfectly captured Beaton's and London's Swinging 'Sixties (Plate 69). Beaton arranged that one area of his archive should not be sold to Sotheby's. He had photographed the British royal family from 1938 to 1970. His many books of press cuttings, which he bequeathed to the Museum's Archive of Art and Design, show how widely and lavishly the royal photographs were published. Beaton bequeathed the royal photographs to his devoted secretary Eileen Hose MBE. Because of Sir Cecil's high regard for Strong and the V&A, Miss Hose in turn bequeathed them to the Photography Collection. In Sir Roy Strong's words 'Cecil Beaton was one of the most potent influences for over forty years on how we visualise the Monarchy. His role as unofficial court photographer came at a crucial moment in the history of the Crown, when the institution had been badly shaken by the abdication crisis. A new and powerful image had to be created to reestablish the mystique of the Royal Family in the eyes of the world as well as presenting it as both human and accessible'.[4] An exhibition was held in honour of the gift in 1986. Beaton's royal portraits are still distributed by his agents Camera Press and income from their use in the media is used, as stipulated in Miss Hose's bequest, 'for the enhancement of the Photography Collection'. Royalties have been used to catalogue the Beaton royal archive, which numbers some 20,000 items, and to improve the storage of the Photography Collection in general. However, in keeping with Beaton's own youthful spirit, funds from the royalties are also used from time to time to acquire works from young photographers.

In the early 1970s the Menil Foundation in Houston, Texas, asked Cartier-Bresson to select a corpus of the most important photographs of his illustrious career. His choice of 385 works was archivally printed in an edition of five sets in 1971–2. Sets belong to Rice University Institute of the Arts, Houston; Osaka University of Arts, Osaka, Japan; the Bibliothèque Nationale, Paris, and the V&A. This major acquisition was exhibited at the Edinburgh Festival in 1978, with other showings at

69. Sir Cecil Beaton (British, 1904–80). **Twiggy (Foale & Tuffin fashion)**, 1967. Gelatin-silver print. 11 1⁄8 × 7 3⁄4 in (29 × 20 cm). Bought 1978. Ph.975–1978.

the Side Gallery, Newcastle, the Hayward Gallery, London, and the Walker Art Gallery, Liverpool. The catalogue, published by the Scottish Arts Council, was introduced by Professor Sir Ernst Gombrich. Whereas Carol Hogben had presented Cartier-Bresson in 1969 essentially as the master photojournalist, less than ten years later Sir Ernst wrote of him as an artist *tout court*. Gombrich placed Cartier-Bresson squarely in a humanist tradition traced from Velázquez and the brothers Le Nain.

70. David Bailey (British, born 1938). **Mick Jagger**, 1964. Gelatin-silver print. 19 × 19 in (48.2 × 48.2 cm). Given by the photographer, 1983. Ph.165–1983.

The Museum exhibited *Photographs by Don McCullin* in 1981 and the photographer generously gave the whole exhibition of 120 prints to the collection. McCullin had personally printed them for the occasion. Some 45,000 visitors saw the exhibition, which included a large selection of the print media in which McCullin's work first appeared. Exhibits included a front-page story, with seven photographs, from the *New York Times* for 28 February 1968 – 'Life and Death in an Ancient Asian City: scenes in the long fight for Hue'. Another exhibit was McCullin's haunting poster from the Biafra war, which he had flyposted over Hampstead Garden Suburb – then a residence of Prime Minister Harold Wilson – in anger at the British Government in 1970. A complete *Sunday Times Magazine* issue was 'exploded', showing every page from front to back cover. The story chosen was one of McCullin's most sustained photo-essays, 'Vietnam: old glory, young blood' (24 March 1968). This showed the complexities and ironies involved in presenting serious photojournalism – at considerable length – in a consumer magazine. McCullin's work was presented as part of a magazine ensemble, even though the magazine projected him as its star. The display revealed the skill and commitment of the magazine's designers at the height of its reputation. They kept his images away from intrusive advertising for spread after spread. The display also demonstrated the power of the 'four-colour blacks' used in the printing (with red or purple underneath the blacks).

Britain's most harrowingly eloquent photographer of war and crisis was followed by another star, Beaton's natural successor in the worlds of fashion and celebrity portraiture. *David Bailey: Black and White Memories* (covering 1957–69) was shown in 1983. Again, Bailey generously donated his show to the Museum. The gift included the iconic portrait of *Mick Jagger*, enjoying early fame and cult status in 1964 (Plate 70). The assured Jagger, bathed in studio light as a parka-haloed Mod, contrasts with Roger Mayne's street-wary Teds from 1956 (Plate 59). Strong described Bailey's work as 'one of the major points of visual reference for the period'.[5] The exhibition was introduced by Dr David Alan Mellor of the University of Sussex, Britain's leading specialist on the 'Sixties. Mellor emphasized the shift in status represented by Bailey's career:

> To Cecil Beaton, writing a homage to Bailey in 1963, the young photographer personified the triumph of the profession, 'a tremendous advance' in terms of status. The photographer had been 'a sort of inferior tradesman... But now photographers can go anywhere'.[6]

Contact with Bailey led to an ambitious project, sponsored by Olympus Cameras. The historian of fashion photography, Martin Harrison, worked with Bailey for two years to produce *Shots of Style: Great Fashion Photographs Chosen by David Bailey* (1986). This was in the tradition of Bill Brandt's selection *The Land: 20th Century Landscape Photographs* in 1975. As with *The Land*, the Museum collected as many of the exhibits as possible. Thus, the Museum acquired classic – and not so well known – photographs by Richard Avedon, Gianpaolo Barbieri, Lillian Bassman, Adolphe de Meyer, Louise Dahl-Wolfe, Arthur Elgort, Hiro, Frank Horvat, William Klein, Barry Lategan, Peter Lindbergh, Genevieve Naylor, Helmut Newton, Jean-Loup Sieff, Melvin Sokolsky, Bert Stern and Bruce Weber, as well as further works by Man Ray and Edward Steichen. Because of the Museum's great collection of costume, fashion photography has continued to receive special emphasis. The John French Archive was given by Vere French in 1979 (and is now, like the Museum's extensive collection of Worth photographs, housed in the Archive of Art and Design). *Appearances: Fashion Photography since 1945* was curated by Martin Harrison in 1991. This show and book deliberately placed fashion photography within the wider context of style and the history of photography generally. The project led to acquisitions by Walker Evans, Louis Faurer, Robert Frank and other photographers outside the canon of fashion. In 1977 *Contemporary Fashion Photography* was shown, selected by Charlotte Cotton, Assistant Curator of Photographs. Acquisitions in this area have continued to receive generous support from Olympus Cameras and leading photographers in the field.

Roger Mayne, on hearing of the new dispensation for photography at the V&A in 1977, immediately offered to donate the original book 'dummy' of his best known series: *Portrait of Southam Street, 1956–61*. He had hoped to publish this fine work, containing 80 photographs, as a book in the early 1960s. His intense, observant and poetic portrait resulted from five years of visits to one street in London's W10 (Notting Dale) district. The series was finally published in book form by the V&A in 1986 and exhibited with spectacular success. Many of the children photographed in the 1950s came to the exhibition opening, bringing children of their own. The exhibition was simultaneously local, national and photographic history.

By the 1980s the 1950s had become a 'black hole' in British photographic history. Major figures, such as Bill Brandt's friend and supporter Norman Hall, had died. Brandt himself died in 1983. The Museum had been working closely with him on an exhibition which became a memorial to his passing. The opening of *Bill Brandt's 'Literary Britain'* (1984) was marked by tributes to the great photographer from Sir Tom Hopkinson and Sue Davies. The show was made up almost entirely of vintage prints from Brandt's own collection. He disliked the low tonal contrast of the prints he had made for reproduction in magazines and books from the 1930s into the early 1950s. He much preferred the larger ('drawing-room size', in his phrase) and highly contrasty prints that he made, or had made for him, from about 1960. However,

Figure 11. JOHN DEAKIN (British, 1912–72). **Francis Bacon**, 1952. Gelatin silver print. 14⅞ × 12⅛ in (38.1 x 30.8 cm). Bought 1984. Ph.100–1984.

when told that students liked to see the earlier prints of great photographers, he relented and gave the Photography Collection a small but fascinating group of vintage examples. The group included an exquisite print of his landscape masterpiece *Seagull's Nest, Midsummer's Eve, Isle of Skye* (1947). Like Penn, Brandt had lived successfully and famously beyond the era of his magazine success and into the new world of museums, galleries and the market for photographs.

Other photographers who shone in the 1950s were not so fortunate. The journalist Bruce Bernard proposed an exhibition of the tattered photographic remains of John Deakin, who had photographed brilliantly for *Vogue* in the early 1950s and died in 1972. *John Deakin: The Salvage of a Photographer* was shown in 1984. Francis Bacon, Deakin's friend and the subject of his most famous portrait (Figure 11), paid for the opening party, which was attended by many of Deakin's Soho friends, such as the Bernard brothers and Lucian Freud. Bacon's hospitality was characteristically generous. The painter wrote of Deakin in the catalogue: 'his portraits to me are the best since Nadar and Julia Margaret Cameron'.[7] The Bacon portrait, perfectly and symbolically distressed by chance, was bought from Deakin's friend Elizabeth Smart, author of *By Grand Central Station I Sat Down and Wept* (1966). It has become one of the most reproduced photographs in the Photography Collection. Deakin had exhibited his photographs at David Archer's Soho bookshop in 1956 and Colin MacInnes had written about them with perceptive enthusiasm in *The Times*. His portraiture reflects but also shares the ruthless brilliance of Francis Bacon and Lucian Freud, his great contemporaries of the 'School of London'. However, Deakin became disenchanted with photography, took up painting and did not live to enjoy his subsequent fame. His rehabilitation was completed in 1996 with a National Portrait Gallery exhibition and a monograph by Robin Muir.

Deakin's show was paired with one devoted to Edwin Smith, a painter by vocation who made his living by illustrating – superbly – a stream of articles and books on architecture and landscape published by *The Saturday Book* and Thames and Hudson. According to his widow, the writer Olive Cook, Smith owned only one photographic book. His copy of *Atget: Photographe de Paris* (1930) is sumptuously bound in purple silk, with Atget's name tooled in gold. Olive Cook presented the book to the Photography Collection, plus 70 of Edwin Smith's photographs in 1985.

Raymond Moore (1920–87) trained as a painter at the Royal College of Art from 1947–50 and took up photography in earnest in 1956. Like Mayne, he was stimulated by the *Subjektive Fotografie* publications. His subtle tonal style is much in keeping with Steinert's school. Helmut Gernsheim bought some of the spare semi-abstractions of Moore's early period. Other pictures took in more of the world's circumstantial detail. Moore visited the United States for the first time in 1970 and found rapport with Harry Callahan, Aaron Siskind and Minor White. Like them, he was based in art colleges. He was the photographer of brilliant long vacations, mainly

71. RAYMOND MOORE (British, 1920–87). **Allonby**, 1977. Gelatin-silver print. 6⅞ × 10⅜ in (17.6 × 26.6 cm). Bought from the photographer, 1981. Ph.413–1981.

in Wales, but also in Cyprus and Ireland. He was well represented (by eight works in colour and black and white) in Bill Brandt's *The Land*. The Circulation Department toured a fifteen-frame selection of his work. After retiring from teaching in 1977 Moore made the north-west coast of England, and then the Scottish Borders, his home and his photographic landscape. He and his wife, the photographer Mary Cooper, held workshops for aspiring landscapists – and his growing number of admirers. Moore generally worked, like Lee Friedlander, with a 35mm camera and had – again like Friedlander – the ability to make prints of outstanding tonal subtlety from small negatives. He followed Bill Brandt as the second British photographer to receive a retrospective at the Hayward Gallery (1981). However, if Brandt's photography was the equivalent of a grand piano, Moore's was a clavichord. The subject of *Allonby* (1979) (Plate 71) is elusive, including the intricate behaviour of preoccupied children, the tension of careening lines, and the immensities of air, light, sea and space. Among the works by Moore in the collection is a unique print that he particularly wished the Museum to have. This is relatively large and entitled *Strange Fencing, Blaenau Ffestiniog* (1966) – a skyline fence improvised from decorative iron bedsteads on a Welsh farm. It was illustrated in 1968 on the cover of Moore's Welsh Arts Council exhibition catalogue, when the negative was lost.

The Museum's role as preserver of photography's recent past and vulnerable present was emphasized by a letter to the present writer from South Africa's major photographer David Goldblatt. Goldblatt's sharp-eyed observation of his country under Apartheid was presented in an exhibition of 115 of his photographs, organized by Side Gallery, Newcastle, which toured Britain in the late 1980s. Goldblatt wrote from Johannesburg on 6 January 1987:

> Obstinately, and probably unrealistically, I still believe that this can become as reasonably 'just' a society as can be hoped for, and that the transition to that distant state might happen without catastrophic conflict. Increasingly, however, that belief is becoming baseless. In the face of the awful things happening here and the worse that are very possible it is ridiculous to be concerned with anything so paltry as photographs. But I am. And it seems to me that considering their vulnerability to destruction, it might one day be useful and even valuable to have a fairly wide ranging collection of photographs from South Africa, such as this exhibition, housed outside this country in a museum which is publicly accessible and as likely to be permanent as any institution can be. Hence the V&A.

A selection of the gift was shown in *African Themes* in 1993 with works by the young British artists Faisal Abdu'Allah and Maud Sulter. *Farmer's Son with his Nursemaid, Marico Bushveld*, 1964 (Plate 72) was taken under especially interesting circumstances. Reportage or documentary photography sometimes has startling affinities with fiction.

72. David Goldblatt (South African, born 1930). **Farmer's Son with his Nursemaid, Marico Bushveld**, 1964. Gelatin-silver print. 9 × 13½ in (23 × 34.5 cm). Given by the photographer, 1992. E.12–1992.

73. Chris Killip (British, born 1947). **Rocker and Rosie Going Home, Lynemouth**, 1983. Gelatin-silver print. 16 × 19¾ in (41 × 50.5 cm). Bought from the photographer, 1984. Ph.131–1985.

In the early 1960s Goldblatt discovered the stories of Herman Charles Bosman, set in the remote Western Transvaal Bushveld – to which Goldblatt managed to wangle one of his earliest magazine assignments. Bosman's volumes of stories like *Mafeking Road* and *Unto Dust* told, Goldblatt says, of 'the lives of the Afrikaner bushveld farmers, their black workers and much of what came out of that potent mix... He wrote with deceptive simplicity in the most economic and literate English yet with the idiomatic earthiness of Afrikaans'.[8] Goldblatt found that the Marico Bushveld was full of Bosman echoes. 'He used the real names and lives of the people, simply putting my name on your story and vice versa'.

Goldblatt made his photograph on the farm where Bosman had boarded and taught school in an old barn in the 1920s. The little boy's grandmother was the writer's landlady. Although Bosman provided the location and the occasion of the photograph, its content is very different – and probably rooted in Goldblatt's own upbringing in South Africa. The intimate relationship between the boy and the nursemaid is perfectly shown by the way the girl's hand clasps the child's heel. If the same gesture of physical intimacy had taken place when the boy was grown up, Goldblatt pointed out, an offence would have been committed under the Apartheid laws. Like other intuitive photographers, Goldblatt captured a web of likenesses and contrasts – bare tree/plain boy, beautiful girl/tree in leaf, capped white child/bare-headed black servant, white structure/brown land – presented, of course, in black and white. In 1996 Goldblatt made another gift to the collection – his portrait of President Mandela.

Chris Killip described his book *In Flagrante* (1988) as 'a fiction about metaphor'. The book is a convincing and complicated fiction developed during the 1980s, outside the conventions of photojournalism. Killip managed to piece together a way of living and working in the 1970s and 1980s that typifies 'Independent Photography'. This phrase describes personally initiated rather than commissioned projects. Independent photographers may welcome publication in mass-circulation magazines, or on TV, but work to their own priorities. They are concerned to keep control over the final presentation of their work. Killip's first large-scale series was *Isle of Man: A Book about the Manx*, published with an introduction by John Berger in 1980. The Photography Collection acquired the master set of 69 prints from which the book was printed. Killip's careful examination of the surfaces and subtleties of a way of life takes on greater meaning when viewed over the whole series of prints. His exhibition *In Flagrante* was shown at the Museum in 1988. The Museum simultaneously showed 'The Photographer's Eye' – Killip's selection of works by other photographers. This was mainly drawn from the existing Photography Collection, but some works were acquired especially for the show. These included prints by Jimmy Forsyth, David Goldblatt, Nan Goldin, Martin Parr, John Sturrock and Cindy Sherman. Killip wrote illuminatingly about his choices.

74. Lewis Baltz (American, born 1945). **Prospector Park Subdivision III, Lot 123 Looking North**, from the series **Park City**, published 1980. Gelatin-silver print. 6⅜ × 9½ in (16.3 × 24.3 cm). Anonymous gift, 1983. Ph.285–1983.

Killip's *Rocker and Rosie Going Home, Lynemouth* (1983) was taken at a seacoal gatherers' camp at Lynemouth, Northumberland, where Killip lived and photographed regularly in 1982–4 (Plate 73). The seacoal was not a natural harvest, of course, it was part of the waste jettisoned by a National Coal Board pit and washed ashore. The sea separates coal from the waste. With favourable winds, tides and currents, the coal washes ashore at the seacoalers' beach. Their difficult and chancey trade fascinated Killip and won his admiration – as he won the trust of his subjects. Killip exhibited 70 of the 'Seacoaler' photographs at the Side Gallery, Newcastle in the early months of 1984. *Rocker and Rosie Going Home* was on show when Britain's most testing struggle of loyalties since the General Strike of 1926 had just begun. The Great Coal Strike ran from March 1984 to March 1985, dividing families, communities and the nation at large. Killip's photographs show affection, achievement and aspiration at the most marginal place in the western economy.

Killip's book *In Flagrante*, with text by John Berger and Sylvia Grant, opens and closes with photographs chosen to demonstrate the artificiality of photography. He told the journalist David Lee that he had 'tried to make it obvious from the outset that photographs are not to be trusted. I want people to be conscious of the subjective nature of photography and that a photograph is never objective. Photographs are themselves only a fiction'.[9] Fifteen of the Seacoal photographs were acquired in 1986. Killip later donated a further group of works from *In Flagrante*. Other British 'Independent Photographers' include Killip's close associate Graham Smith, plus other internationally recognized photographers – John Davies, Paul Graham, Ian MacDonald and Martin Parr – all of whom are well represented in the collection. Martin Parr has, in turn, supported younger British photographers and donated their photographs regularly. He also very generously offered to bequeath his outstanding collection of British photographic postcards to the collection. Some examples were exhibited in *Street Photography* in 1994–5.

The United States counterparts of these British photographers include the founders of the 'New Topographics'. This term was coined in 1975 to describe a new take on landscape. The movement's leaders were Robert Adams, Lewis Baltz, Frank Gohlke and John Gossage. Their clear-eyed study of environmental actualities became a worldwide influence and would be especially fruitful in the work of Michael Schmidt in Berlin and Hiromi Tsuchida in Tokyo. All of these photographers are represented in the collection. Lewis Baltz (Plate 74) gave the idea of photography as fiction a different twist when he remarked that 'It might be more useful, if not necessarily more true, to think of photography as a narrow, deep area between the novel and film'.[10] Baltz produced a trilogy of books and exhibitions that began with *The New Industrial Parks near Irvine, California* (1975). Next came *Park City* (1980) and finally *San Quentin Point* (1986). Marvin Heiferman's phrase 'Landscape-as-Real-Estate' is particularly relevant to *Park City*. This is a series of 102 photographs that document the construction of the ski resort of that name a few miles east of Salt Lake City, Utah. The photographs are from 35mm negatives taken with a Leica on a tripod. Printed on cold-toned paper, they dispassionately record construction in the knowledge that it is simultaneously environmental destruction. The series is a factual document of building practice and a larger allegory about values. *Park City* chimes with Joan Didion's essay 'Many Mansions' (1977). Didion reflected on the specific qualities and symbolic properties of 'the new official residence for governors of California, unlandscaped, unfurnished, and unoccupied since the construction stopped in 1975'. The implications of this eloquent shell lead her to conclude: 'I have never seen a house so evocative of the unspeakable'. The nature of 'development' becomes similarly evocative over the 102 stark prints of *Park City*. The series reflects the unrelenting ruthlessness of the commercial exploitation of land that it depicts. Acquired by purchase and anonymous gift in 1983, the complete series was exhibited in 1985.

75. Masahisa Fukase (Japanese, born 1934). From the series **Ravens**, 1975–85. Gelatin-silver print. 8½ × 12¾ in (21.5 × 32.5 cm). Bought from the photographer, 1987. Ph.7203–1987.

Ravens is a cycle of photographs made over a ten-year period by Masahisa Fukase. He is one of a quartet of outstanding Japanese photographers who exhibited as 'The Eyes of Four', the others being Eikoh Hosoe, Daido Moriyama and Shomei Tomatsu. *Ravens* began with a chance photograph of a flock of crows, taken on Fukase's native Hokkaido in 1975. It culminated in a series of 62 photographs published in book form in 1986. The first, taken in a burst of activity in 1975–8, were part of another long and complex work. Fukase's wife Yohko inspired a whole narrative cycle, eventually published in 1978, in which parts of the Crows/Ravens series play an ominous role. Yohko was a Noh performer and the work, essentially dramatic in its juxtapositions, staging and sequencing, was derived from their marriage and, in 1976, divorce. Obsession, melancholy and loss deepen from photograph to photograph, gradually drawing in more and more aspects of modern Japan. The black silhouettes of birds evoke *sumi–e* ink paintings and war planes. The darkness of the book envelops the symbol of technological prowess and efficiency, the Shinkansen or 'Bullet' train (Plate 75). The photographs link across the book through fleeting resemblances, oppositions, repetitions and the pictorial equivalents of assonance and half-rhyme. An earlier version of the series, in the form of 54 prints, and three highly graphic enlargements, was acquired from Masahisa Fukase in 1987 and exhibited in *PHOTOGRAPHY NOW* in 1989.

Fukase's book was acquired by the National Art Library, which has retained photographic publications that include text – works like *The Pencil of Nature* or Emerson's *Life and Landscape on the Norfolk Broads* (1886). Since 1977 the National Art Library has acquired very substantially in the field of photography, including key journals, monographs, early texts, exhibition catalogues and experimental publications. These are supplemented by 'Information Files', on photographers and institutions, containing such material as press cuttings, exhibition announcements, and sometimes

Figure 12. DANNY LYON (American, born 1942). **NOW Poster for the Student Non-Violent Coordinating Committee**, 1963. Offset lithograph. 22⅛ × 14 in (56.1 × 35.5 cm). Bought 1995. E.2740-1995.

correspondence. A major acquisition was the Osman/Gidal collection of newspapers and magazines illustrating the history of photojournalism. This was assembled over many years by Colin Osman, founder of *Creative Camera* in London, and the pioneer photojournalist Tim Gidal in Jerusalem. It is especially strong on the German illustrated magazines of the 1920s, in which the layouts and visual language of mass-circulation photojournalism were invented.

In the Department of Prints, Drawings and Paintings, the Photography Collection is flanked by a broad range of media including miniature, oil and watercolour paintings, prints, posters, designs and illustrations. This spread of interrelated collections can serve the study of photography in valuable ways. For example, Chris Titterington curated *The Pencil of Nature* in 1994 as a fascinating cross-media show. Expert in both the history of watercolours and photography, he brought together photographic and other prints (including 'nature prints' acquired by Cole in 1854), and revealed the profound underlying connections between different processes and techniques.

The spread of connected collections embraces different aspects of the work of the American photographer Danny Lyon. Lyon is represented by 30 prints in the Photography Collection, a range of exhibition catalogues and other publications plus an information file in the National Art Library, and five posters published by the Student Non-Violent Coordinating Committee during the Civil Rights Movement of the late 1960s. These were recently acquired from Lyon for the Prints Collection (Figure 12). Lee Friedlander is represented by 28 gelatin-silver prints and 24 photogravures, plus examples of his fine limited edition books in the National Art Library.

The Photography Collection has been cared for by many hands, known and unknown, over nearly 150 years. Within the Department, cataloguing has advanced dramatically in the last two decades, helped by generations of student volunteers. In addition, Virginia Dodier received a two-year Getty Trust Grant to catalogue Lady Hawarden's photographs. Her invaluable catalogue raisonné, completed in 1989 and available for study in the Print Room, was followed by a retrospective exhibition, which she curated. *Clementina, Lady Hawarden – Photographer* was shown at the V&A in 1989 and afterwards toured, through the British Council, to the Musée d'Orsay, Paris, The Museum of Modern Art, New York and the J. Paul Getty Museum, Malibu. Another remarkable cataloguing project was undertaken by Michael Wigg, a student on the new MA course in the history of photography and society at the London Institute, who catalogued some 6,000 photographs by Francis Frith & Co., donated in 1953–4. Exceptionally among museums in Britain, the V&A has a conservator of photographs, since 1981, who is supported by the Conservation Department's Science Section. The photographs of paintings returned from Essex University in 1996. New storage has been built for the large-scale works typical of today, and low-temperature storage is now available to house the increasing number of works produced in colour materials.

Walker Evans memorably remarked, with help from a witty typographer: 'Colour tends to corrupt photography and absolute colour corrupts it absolutely. Consider the way colour film usually renders blue sky, green foliage, lipstick red, and the kiddies's playsuit. There are four simple words for the matter, which must be whispered: colour photography is vulgar'. Evans allowed one exception: 'When the point of a picture subject is precisely its vulgarity or its colour-accident through man's hands not God's, then only can colour film be used validly'.[11] Thus, even after the larger doubts about the medium had receded, colour photography had its own special problems of acceptance – for understandable reasons. While a skilled photographer could control the tonalities of black and white prints, colour values remained relatively arbitrary and unruly. To adapt the metaphor of photography as shooting, to use colour instead of black and white was to trade a rifle for a shotgun. The crucial exhibition was *William Eggleston's Guide*, curated by John Szarkowski and shown at The Museum of Modern Art, New York in 1976. A furore followed. The burden of the general reproof was that Eggleston's *Guide* was the art of the snapshot, and that was no art at all.

However, in time both Eggleston and Szarkowski were vindicated. The photographs have been widely exhibited and finely published. Eggleston had studied the possibilities of colour photography more acutely than any one else and found a solution to the problem of control. As a young man he had greatly admired, and constantly tried to emulate, Cartier-Bresson. The problem was that Cartier-Bresson had mainly photographed in Europe, the Orient and black and white. Eggleston found himself, as he explained in an interview, leaving out of his photographs everything that was characteristic of his native landscape in the American South. When he recognized the absurdity of this he decided how to photograph the Southern spirit of place. Perhaps taking Walker Evans's remarks to heart, Eggleston used colour film to photograph the new shopping centres going up around Memphis, Tennessee. He recalled the scene much later: 'all the trees had been cut, architecture just barely could be called architecture'. He found his first colour photographs 'perfectly satisfactory'.[12] Eggleston found a way to control the colour and to saturate it. Just as fine artists had begun to use the commercial, silkscreen process in the 1960s, Eggleston worked with craftsmen of the dye-transfer technique. Dye transfer was primarily used to manipulate advertising material. Eggleston used 35mm colour transparency film, a Leica (sometimes on a tripod), and the dye-transfer process to create a new world for photography. Like Raymond Moore before him, his subject is the 'uncommonness of the commonplace' (Plate 76). As part of his study of colour, Eggleston spent hours at photographic printing labs, watching 'the continuous ribbon of small, oblong images... Maybe at one minute we might see twelve or fifteen pictures that two people made on their first trip after having been married, and they forgot to have them developed. And years later (in fact, the day before) they sent them over, and here I was looking at them. Next to those, without a break, might have been something taken the night before by someone's children celebrating some kind of event, a family event (let's say). Luckily (I think, at least, from my point of view) I wasn't plagued with having to watch any work taken for commercial reasons (that I remember), any work where someone was told to set this or that picture up. It was one of the most exciting and unforgettable experiences as a whole – and educational for me.'[13] He used the experience to make photographs that capture the everyday and the overlooked, and reveal it – for a moment – as glorious and splendid. *William Eggleston: Colour Photographs of the American South* was shown at the V&A in 1983. Colour photography began, at last, to become as familiar in galleries as it was in the households of amateurs.

Whereas Eggleston uses a Leica camera, usually hand-held, Joel Sternfeld has typically worked with a plate camera on a tripod. His photograph of the *Exhausted Renegade Elephant, Washington State* 1979, (Plate 77) is replete with exact physical

76. William Eggleston (American, born 1937). **Sink, St Simon's Island**, 1978. Dye-transfer print. 10⅛ × 15¼ in (26.8 × 38.6 cm). Bought 1981. Ph.245–1981.

TROPICANA

description from the leaves of the pines to the fawn trouser-leg in the sheriff's car. The camera is positioned above and slightly away from the main point of interest. Sternfeld takes in everything like an independent witness. The viewer is presented with abundant information but probably remains as puzzled as the bystanders in the picture. The gaze is attracted to the distant focus of action, moving in closer to interpret the event. Are they pacifying the elephant by spraying it with water? How can they possibly haul it onto the truck? The photograph is as involving as sophisticated advertising and as uncomfortable as involuntary rubbernecking. This scene of confusion under a clear blue sky is surely a symbolic landscape, filled with questions about man's relation to the animal kingdom. Colour photography, so entertainingly mocked by Walker Evans, has been technically and aesthetically refined by photographers of the calibre of Eggleston, Sternfeld and others. Although major work is still being achieved in black and white, colour increasingly became the medium of first choice for many practitioners during the 1980s and 1990s – as we shall see in the next chapter.

77. Joel Sternfeld (American, born 1947). **Exhausted Renegade Elephant, Woodland, Washington State**, 1979. C-type print (1982). 14 1/16 × 18 in (35.8 × 45.8 cm) Bought 1984. Ph.122–1984.

SHERIFF

La Soupe
de
Daguerre

CHAPTER EIGHT

Fond Wrestlers with Photography

When photography was first invented by Talbot and Daguerre, the first practitioners of 'the New Art' came – as they had to – from other fields. Daguerre was Europe's great exponent of the Diorama, which anticipated the spectacular illusions of cinema. Talbot came from a class that cultivated science at the highest level and was familiar with great pictures. Who knows the origins or fate of the enigmatic M. de Ste Croix, whose visit to England in the Autumn of 1839 caused such excitement? Among the first photographers were businessmen/inventors like Claudet. Others had trained – like Anna Atkins, Francis Bedford or Charles Thurston Thompson – in disciplines upon which the new medium dramatically improved. Naturally, many came from the mother art of painting, including such early leaders as Roger Fenton and Gustave Le Gray. Others, however, had declared no great aptitude in the visual media before photography released their gifts. This was the case with such originals as Lady Hawarden and Mrs Cameron. These are all among the splendid figures met, if sometimes only briefly, in the early chapters of this book.

Photography remained hospitable to talents from elsewhere through its 150-year history, but its most recent decades are arguably more like its earliest than any in between. Have there ever been so many creative talents involved with the medium? They come from every discipline and point of view. As we shall see, photography is now used for anything its artists wish to represent – and artists may now represent anything. This is also a time of imaginative and literate commentators, including poets and novelists, philosophers and cultural critics. The preceding chapters have mentioned some, if by no means all, of the principal names. More photographic history has been written in the last 25 years than in the previous 125. There are also more historians and curators. The historians range from devoted amateurs to dedicated doctoral students. There has certainly never been such an abundance of exhibitions and books, and let us not forget the receptive creative work done by the audiences of these exhibitions and publications. As Thomas Crow reminded us recently, there is – despite allegations to the contrary – a large audience for art that is demanding and difficult.[1]

As we have seen, the Museum staged its first international exhibition of contemporary photography in 1858. The second was part of photography's 150th birthday celebrations in 1989. *PHOTOGRAPHY NOW*, sponsored by Agfa, was the Museum's largest and most complex photographic exhibition. Spread over four

78. Marcel Broodthaers (Belgian, 1924–76). **La Soupe de Daguerre**, 1975. Twelve C-type colour photographs mounted on board measuring 20¾ × 20½ in (53 × 52 cm); individual prints 3⅛ × 4⅝ in (8 × 12 cm). Bought 1980. Ph.253–1979.

galleries, it drew 109,954 visitors. Dirk Nishen Verlag, Berlin, published the book of the show, in English and German editions, in association with the V&A. The exhibition simultaneously displayed and undermined stereotypes. It showed a full-size billboard advertisement for cigarettes *and* works by John Baldessari and Richard Prince that questioned the role and power of advertising, and played with its ideas. The show presented glamour and anti-glamour, the commercial and the critical. The most frequently published pictures from the show were, on the one hand, the now widely exhibited reportage by Sebastiao Salgado from the Sierra Pelada goldmine in Brazil; and, on the other, the postmodern satires on celebrity by William Wegman, involving the wonder dog Fay Ray (frontispiece).

79. Helen Chadwick (British, 1953–96). **The Oval Court**, 1986. Mixed media installation. Bought 1988–9. E.1(1-222) 1988.

In 1970 an essay by the anthropologist Edmund Carpenter, an associate of Marshall McLuhan, appeared in a book by the photojournalist Ken Heyman. The book was called *They Became What They Beheld*. Carpenter wrote about the arrival of television as the new dominant medium in the 1960s, a subject touched upon in chapter six. His remarks seem prophetic and true:

> The appearance of any new medium leads to a shift in media ratios, recasting the roles of all older media. Every culture has a primary medium for the classification of that culture's basic clichés. When a new medium replaces it, the old one is freed and takes up its role as a declassifier. The coming of writing enabled one to say what could not be written, and with the coming of print, one could write what couldn't be printed. The coming of films freed the stage for new & bolder drama, just as the appearance of TV freed films.
>
> The older medium is thus free to play a subversive role, much favoured by artists but deplored by those accustomed to speak with the voice of authority.[2]

He also noted that *Life* and the *New York Times*, dethroned by television, had assumed more critical roles. As if to prove his point, in the year after Carpenter's essay appeared, the *New York Times* published 'The Pentagon Papers', which exposed the duplicity of government at the highest level and helped to bring about American withdrawal from Vietnam.

The new freedom of photography attracted free spirits. Among them was a Belgian poet who became a photographer, film-maker, curator of an imaginary museum, maker of miraculous objects – and London resident. Marcel Broodthaers was born in 1924 and died in mid-career in 1976. One of his last and most enchanting works is *La Soupe de Daguerre* (1975) (Plate 78). It was part of a portfolio of 'Multiple Originals' titled *Artists & Photographs*. The portfolio featured a striking range of artists working with the photographic medium: John Baldessari, Bernd and Hilla Becher, Broodthaers himself, Jan Dibbets, Ed Ruscha, Ger van Elk and William Wegman. It was bought in 1979 to form a valuable bridge between prints and photographs in the newly constituted department. In the same year was shown the

exhibition *Photography in Printmaking* (1979), which emphasized the creative links across media characteristic of the time, and exhibited works by Broodthaers and others.

Michael Compton, who introduced the Tate Gallery's *Marcel Broodthaers* exhibition in 1980, wrote of the artist's constant subversion of received or obvious ideas. Perhaps responding to American Pop Art and high-pressure commercial galleries, Broodthaers liked 'to parody the tendency to oversimplify or polarise positions. His method was to bring back into the visual arts the rich, cultural and social heritage of Europe'.[3] Broodthaers presented his work, Compton added, 'as a kind of puzzle; it requires to be solved but cannot be solved. It is in the experience of trying to sort it out and of knowing, finally, that one has not, that one perceives a kind of hidden message'.[4]

Looking at the delicious ingredients of *La Soupe de Daguerre* one might observe that photography keeps everything absolutely fresh. As well as the carefully taken photographs of fresh vegetables, the ensemble includes a shoal of freshwater fish and a solitary pike. To be more exact, we have colour photographs of tissue cut-outs printed in colours representing fish. They look as flavoursome as the tomatoes, but perhaps part of the point is that we read all the ingredients – across forms of representation – as real. At the base is a silkscreened *trompe l'oeil* label, in parody of museum methodology. Does the piece celebrate the creative continuity of past and present, the nimbleness of imagination in leaping apparent divides, or the richness of the pictorial stock? Each viewer will decide on an interpretation – to taste – remembering that this artist is like a butterfly and that his daughter's name is Marie-Puck.

Another Puckish and, alas, short-lived artist of this era was Helen Chadwick (1953–96). Born of English and Greek parentage, Chadwick combined Punk era frankness with a stern perfectionism. The Museum has the world's largest holding of the works that she made using photocopy and photography. *One Flesh* (1985), representing a madonna, a (female) child and a placenta, is a collage of 'photocopies from life' in her phrase. It was bought in 1986 and shown in the the exhibition *Towards a Bigger Picture* in 1987, and afterwards in the Museum's exhibition *The Nude: A New Perspective*, curated by Gill Saunders, in 1989. The Museum's second purchase from Chadwick was *Vanitas* (1986), an installation contrasting (photocopied) fine curtains and firm flesh with tattered cloth and bones. Helen Chadwick broke through to a large audience and national attention for the first time with her exhibition *Of Mutability* at the ICA in 1986. She was short-listed for the Tate Gallery's Turner Prize. After touring in the United Kingdom and to continental Europe, the major part of this installation – *The Oval Court* – was bought by the V&A. It was shown at the Museum as part of *PHOTOGRAPHY NOW* in 1989 (Plate 79). This view was made for the artist at the time by her long-time photographer Edward Woodman at the ICA. The work had its genesis in an architectural tour that Chadwick made with her friend

80. Helen Chadwick (British, 1953–96). **The Oval Court**. Photocopies from life (detail), 1986. Bought 1988–9.E.1(1)-1988.

Philip Stanley to the rococo pilgrimage churches of Bavaria. She wrote:

> It was just before Easter, and there was still plenty of snow… In Die Wies everything inside dissolves, you're in a space that defies architecture, that melts. I saw the melting snow outside, the melting stucco inside, as allegory: the church is dedicated to a statue that wept, and the rocaille wasn't just a decorative device, but related to the thaw and the landscape and the Passion, to the melting of the snow at Easter, and to rebirth.[5]

81. KAREN KNORR (American, British resident, born 1954). **The New Justine**, 1995. Dye destruction print. 36 × 7 15/16 in (91.3 × 66 cm). Given by the photographer, 1996. E.518-1997.

Chadwick's *Gesamtkunstwerk* was itself a thawing-out of pre-Modern traditions for the use of late twentieth-century artists. It was also a spectacular rebirth for the artist herself. *The Oval Court* was largely made with the most basic form of photography/printmaking: an office photocopying machine. This had a toning device which allowed a range of colours. However, the work was always intended to be blue. Chadwick created an imaginary pool filled with swimming bodies, and attributes such as birds, fishes and animals – everything photocopied piece by piece and collaged into position, as shown in the detail in Plate 80. Five spheres, covered with gold leaf, float upon the pool. High on the wall are weeping heads, based on instant passport photos. Leaves stream down the walls like tears, flow through the (computer-drawn) Salomonic columns and join the blue waters. Here, Marina Warner has written:

> we enter into a post-lapsarian Paradise where woman is visible alone among humankind, where she is the matter in question, but what matters is her passion, her physical articulation of her feelings, her relation to created things and her choice among them; where her aloneness is not an issue and absence not felt, as was the lack of woman felt by Adam. We are introduced into a cycle of experiences, mediated through an imaginary body composed from the artist's own, from photocopies in collage. *'I want to catch the physical sensations passing across the body – sensations of gasping, yearning, breathing, fullness,'* says the artist. *'The bodies are bearing their sexuality like a kind of Aeolian harp, through which the sensations are drifting and playing. Each of them is completely swollen up with pleasure at the moment when it's about to turn, each has reached the pitch of plenitude before it starts to decay, to empty…'*[6]

The language that Marina Warner used in her eloquent appreciation of *The Oval Court* anticipates the terms in which new accounts of Lady Hawarden would be written soon afterwards. The preoccupations of the 1980s and 1990s illuminate the 1850s and 1860s. Lady Hawarden has become the most studied photographer in the collection. Ingrid Sischy has written that the photographs of Lady Hawarden's daughters are about a highly elusive and original subject: the 'moods and thoughts… the interior life of the girls'.[7] Helen Grace Barlow sees the photographs as 'discrete images of the multiple emotions that constitute character'. Hawarden uses mirrors to subversive

effect 'because the mirror, like the photograph, displays a disconcerting capacity to present the viewer with a completely unknown aspect of an apparently familiar object'.[8]

'I respect photography', Helen Chadwick remarked, but she didn't care for 'the fetishization of technique'. She described herself as 'a fond wrestler with photography'.[9] By using photocopy she was able to suggest bodies touching water, simultaneously real and withheld. She called these images 'echoes off the body'. Like Broodthaers, Chadwick helped to re-establish the vast repertoire of European iconography for artists of her generation.

The V&A worked with the Department of the Environment in 1987–8 to commission artists to make works in the national parks. Helen Chadwick produced her first computer-edited photographic series *Viral Landscapes*. One of these, *Viral Landscape No.2* was later bought for the collection and exhibited in *Graphic Responses to AIDS* in 1996.

Partly as a conscious reminiscence of Julia Margaret Cameron's work at the South Kensington Museum in the 1860s, five artists were invited to make new work at the V&A as part of *PHOTOGRAPHY NOW*. The Polaroid Corporation provided a 20 × 24 in camera and their skilled technician, Jan Hnizdos. The artists were Sue Arrowsmith, Zarina Bhimji, Helen Chadwick, Hannah Collins and Roberta Graham. They worked partly in public hours, when visitors could watch and talk to them, and partly in private. Their work was shown as an instant exhibition and the prints shared between the artists, the Polaroid Collection and the Museum. Chadwick's *Meat Lamps*, made on this occasion, became widely exhibited.[10]

In 1992 she gave the Museum a collection of the preparatory drawings and photocopies for *The Oval Court*. She valued the V&A enormously as an archive. It was typical of Helen Chadwick that she spent part of 15 March 1996 in the Print Room at the V&A, studying the rococo silk designs of Anna-Maria Garthwaite. Her heart stopped, for reasons unknown, later that day.

This was, of course, a period of many untimely deaths. *PHOTOGRAPHY NOW* included a work greatly admired by Chadwick, Robert Mapplethorpe's *Mercury* (1987), lent to the exhibition by Harry H. Lunn Jr.[11] This is a unique platinum print on linen representing a Roman marble, flanked by a fabric panel of Imperial purple. *Mercury* was an oblique and eloquent elegy for the generation who had died of AIDS, like Mapplethorpe's lover Sam Wagstaff, or were dying, like Mapplethorpe himself. *Mercury* was on show at the time of Mapplethorpe's own death in March 1989.

Three earlier works had been bought from Mapplethorpe in 1980: *Bob Love (Nude)* (1979), *Patti Smith with Doves* (1979) and *Elaine Mayes* (1980). The seated nude of Bob Love could, like the 1855 nude by John Watson (Plate 14), be called an 'Academic Study' – through Sam Wagstaff, Mapplethorpe was deeply familiar with nineteenth-century photography.

82. ROTIMI FANI-KAYODE (Nigerian, worked Britain, 1955–89). **Nothing to lose XII (Bodies of Experience)**, 1989. Dye destruction print (1996). 19½ × 19½ in (49.5 × 49.5 cm). Bought 1996. E.1084–1996.

Karen Knorr, who has maintained the tradition of artists working in the V&A, has also made impressive use of marble sculptures in her work and continues the cosmopolitan theme of this chapter. Born in Germany of American parents, and brought up in Puerto Rico, New Hampshire, Switzerland and France, she was taught by Victor Burgin in 1977–80 at the Central London Polytechnic (now the University of Westminster) and has been a British resident ever since. For her series *Connoisseurs*, Knorr made a piece in the Museum's Cast Court titled *The Work of Art in the Age of Mechanical Reproduction* (1994). She has generously presented prints of works photographed in the Museum to the collection. Knorr subsequently worked in the Museum with video and made further photographs featuring Neoclassical sculptures. *The New Justine* (1995) (Plate 81) is based on *Helen of Troy* (1825–7) by John Gibson (1791–1866) and is part of a series entitled *The Virtues and the Delights*, begun in 1992. As the rococo was for Helen Chadwick, so the Enlightenment is for Karen Knorr. Her epigraph for *The Virtues and the Delights* is taken from Immanuel Kant: 'Sapere aude. Have courage to use your own understanding: that is the motto of the Enlightenment'.[12] The series interprets the Enlightenment 'as an unfinished project, which promotes the secular principle of human perfectibility, where human beings are affirmed as active agents in determining their own independence and futures.' In particular, the series celebrates those feminist thinkers of marble clarity and finesse who opposed the patriarchal underpinnings of the Enlightenment, 'demanding a vital place for women in setting the agenda for life in the "Cities of the Future".' The cast of the series includes Voltaire and De Sade 'as fellow travellers in dispute with contemporary views of women and nature. Emilie du Châtelet, Louise d'Epinay and Mary Wollstonecraft are voices which protest Rousseau's view of women [as] created for man's delight.' *The Virtues and the Delights* is a form of history writing, both a vindication and a celebration of the cultural achievements and intellectual rights of women. Knorr's predecessor, Mrs Cameron, photographed through the decade in which John Stuart Mill wrote *On the Subjection of Women*, but she died 50 years before British women were allowed to vote.

The New Justine takes its title from the novel by the Marquis de Sade. *La Nouvelle Justine, ou les Malheurs de la Vertu* (1797) recounts the misadventures of a paragon of human nature, whose goodness and innocence are abused at every turn. De Sade's terrifying tale (which does, indeed, reflect the Terror) is a riposte to the sentimentality of Rousseau's *La Nouvelle Héloise*. Knorr's *New Justine* belongs to our time – in which sacred statues apparently weep blood, women's rights are major politics and appropriate software harmlessly transforms Museum masterpieces. This work, and the earlier series, *Connoisseurs*, also highlights another of Knorr's preoccupations: 'The white statue epitomizes a certain Eurocentric/Aryan view of Beauty that represses colour'. Knorr took an MA in photographic studies at the University of Derby in 1988–90. One of her fellow students, Maud Sulter, whose

83. Maud Sulter (British, born 1960). **Terpsichore**, 1989. Dye destruction print. 47½ × 37½ in (120 × 95 cm). Bought 1992. E.1795–1991.

work we shall also meet in this chapter, powerfully developed this theme.

Rotimi Fani-Kayode was born in Lagos, Nigeria in 1955 and studied photography at the Pratt Institute in New York before coming to live and work in London. He became a founder-member of Autograph – The Association of Black Photographers – and published *Black Male/White Male* in 1988. He experimented with colour photography of the black nude, using symbols and ideas derived from his native Nigeria. His chose a taboo subject: the homoerotic desire of black men (Plate 82). The work he made with his partner Alex Hirst was exhibited and published in the exhibition and book *Ecstatic Antibodies* (1990), curated/edited by Tessa Boffin and Sunil Gupta. He exhibited widely until his death (not from AIDS) in 1989. No doubt the vigorous colour and iconographic originality of Fani-Kayode's work derived from Nigerian traditions that he knew well, but perhaps his work gained strength from the transformation of the arts in London during the 1980s. His work may reflect, say, the sensationally erotic dance of Michael Clark and the luscious cinematography of Derek Jarman's *Caravaggio* (1987).

Maud Sulter was born in Glasgow of Scots and Ghanaian parentage in 1960. She is a poet, historian, teacher and artist – working with installation, photography and video. She participated in the notable exhibition *The Thin Black Line* at the ICA in 1985. Sulter produced *Zabat* as a response to the celebration of the 150th anniversary of photography in 1989 as an overwhelmingly white occasion. She was then artist-in-residence at Rochdale Art Gallery, where *Zabat* was first shown (1989). It is a remarkable cycle of studio portraits of creative black women, each representing one of the nine muses of classical antiquity. An artist's book, *Zabat: Poetics of a Family Tree* (1989), expands on the iconography of the series. A portrait of the novelist Alice Walker represents Thalia, muse of comedy. A remark by Alice Walker, quoted as an epigraph to the text on Clio, muse of history, illuminates the whole series with sharp humour: 'As a black person and a woman I don't read history for facts, I read it for clues'.

Terpsichore, muse of the dance, is represented by a portrait of Delta Streete, a performance artist (Plate 83). This kind of period-costume portrait may remind some viewers of Cindy Sherman's skewed recapitulations of the iconography and wardrobes of the Old Masters. Eighteenth-century costume also appears in the influential work of Victor Burgin. However, the rationale of the costume here is very specific. Sulter's text meditates on the role of black servants in eighteenth-century Britain. She describes a black servant modelling the gown of her white mistress for a portrait. She recalls the portrayal of black servants as chattels in family portraits, and how they were painted-out in post-Slavery times. The quartz in the model's hand is the 'fool's gold' of sugar cane and crack. The series leads into many stories, but the meaning of *Terpsichore* is also visible at one glance. The much put-upon black sister *will* be going to the ball.

84. Nan Goldin (American, born 1953). **Jimmy Paulette on David's Bike, NYC**, 1991. Dye destruction print. 30 × 40 in (70.2 × 101.7 cm) Bought 1997. E.53-1977.

Sir Roy Strong left the Museum after fourteen years as Director in 1987. Major photographic acquisitions – embracing the whole history – continued under his successor, Dame Elizabeth Esteve-Coll (Director, 1988–1995). These included *The Oval Court* and *Zabat*. The last large photography show of her directorship was *Warworks: Women, Photography and the Art of War* (1995). This was curated for the Museum by Val Williams and Anna Fox. The tight budgets of recent times have resulted in complex partnerships between institutions. The costs of shipping large works and preparing them for exhibition were met by joining forces with the Dutch Institute of Photography in Rotterdam and the South Bank Centre in London (which toured the exhibition in England, Scotland and Wales). Virago published the book by Val Williams and the show finished at the Museum of Contemporary Photography in Ottawa.

85. Annette Lemieux (American, born 1957). **Apparition**, 1989. C-type print. 18 × 12¼ in (45.7 × 31 cm). Bought 1992. E.332–1994.

War photography is almost always reportage, but *Warworks* offered many other possibilities. The exhibition is represented by a group of acquisitions for the permanent collection. The cast was international: Ania Bien from Amsterdam, Hannah Collins from Barcelona, Anna Fox from London, Moira McIver from Belfast, Sophie Ristelhueber from Paris and – from a variety of locations in the United States – Barbara Alpers, Deborah Bright, Masumi Hayashi, Anne Noggle, Sophie Ristelhueber, Martha Rosler and Judith Joy Ross. This was war as the sexy glamour of redcoats' uniforms inhabited by vulnerable contemporary flesh, war remembered as old trench patterns in the fields of Flanders becoming new tourist sites, war as the crumbling concentration camps for Japanese Americans, war as a male narrative in which female fliers are forgotten, war as television from Vietnam making nightmares in the sitting-room, war as whatever is imagined by teenagers at the Vietnam Veterans Memorial, war on the Gulf Channel, war as weekend recreation and war as Holocaust.

The work of Nan Goldin (Plate 84) was originally seen by audiences in Europe and the United States in the form of slide shows with a rock-and-soul soundtrack. The shows became one of the most influential books of the time, *The Ballad of Sexual Dependency* (1986). In the words of Katherine Dieckmann, writing in *The Village Voice* for 18 May 1993: 'Ballad supplied the ultimate expression of a certain form of hard living and even harder loving in lower Manhattan and sympathetic points beyond; it both sealed off and celebrated the moment right before AIDS began its most vicious devastation. The book's uncompromising images of junkies, clubbers, and battered sweethearts have only gained resonance in retrospect.' They are resonant because of Goldin's intimate involvement with and commitment to her 'subjects', but also because of her sheer skill as a colour photographer. Her influence grows out of her twenty-year dedication to a scene which was moving from underground to the street as she photographed it. The sympathetic points beyond, referred to above, naturally included London, where Nan Goldin shot some of the photographs for the book. In London, the sexual revolution was also a style revolution. It was led from the street,

rather than by couturiers. The largest museum exhibition on this theme was *Street Style: From Sidewalk to Catwalk*, directed by Ted Polhemus, shown at the V&A in 1994–5. The research for this event led to acquisitions for the Photography Collection of images of youth subcultures and styles by Della Grace, Leo Reagan and Wolfgang Tillmans.

Nan Goldin's photographs have been influential both internationally and across genres and – as if Martin Harrison had perfectly predicted it with his exhibition *Appearances* in 1991 – British fashion photography in the 1990s meshed with a knowing irony and informal realism. Key players include the photographers Corinne Day, Glen Luchford, Jurgen Teller and Donna Trope, whose works have recently been acquired for the collection, and the magazines *Dazed and Confused* and *I–D*. Annette Lemieux, like Nan Goldin and many other distinguished photographic artists, took part in one of the most heartening events of the time. The exhibition *The Indomitable Spirit* was organized by Photographers + Friends United Against AIDS. It was presented at the International Center of Photography Midtown gallery in Manhattan early in 1990 and then at the Los Angeles Municipal Art Gallery. Ninety-four photographs donated by their makers were auctioned at Sotheby's in New York on Sunday, 14 October 1990. Among them was a black and white photograph by Annette Lemieux titled *Meeting One's Maker* (1989). This image was also presented by Lemieux as a colour image titled *Apparition*, from the same year (Plate 85). The elegiac quality of the gelatin-silver print was changed by the presence of colour. Colour charges the dream-like qualities of the image with contemporaneity – living contact between the well and the damaged. *Apparition* became part of a portfolio of images, also titled *The Indomitable Spirit*, produced by Photographers + Friends United Against AIDS in 1989 (acquired in 1994). Its successor, titled IN A DREAM YOU SAW A WAY TO SURVIVE AND YOU WERE FULL OF JOY, a text by Jenny Holzer, was published in 1991 and bought in 1992.

Another new element in the 1990s is the intimate photography of working-class domestic life by Anthony Haughey, Nick Waplington and others working in colour. Richard Billingham (born 1970) began photographing his family when he first went to art school to do a foundation course in 1990. He photographed the daily round and some serious complications. Robert Yates interviewed him and told his story in *The Observer* on 31 March 1996. Billingham remarked that 'Every day when I came home from college, I used to wonder whether my dad was alive or dead'. Ray, his alcoholic father, was usually drunk, often unconscious. Yates comments: 'while the sight never failed to make him anxious, he started to see Ray's body in another light: "Watching him lying there, I started to think in terms of composition," he says. "So I took photographs to preserve the image"'. When Billingham moved on to study fine art at the University of Sunderland, he continued to photograph his family – partly with the idea of painting from them, perhaps for other reasons. He spoke to Yates about his

86. RICHARD BILLINGHAM (British, born 1970). Untitled (from **Ray's a Laugh** series), 1995. R-type colour print. 47½ × 31½ in (120.6 × 80 cm). Bought 1996. E.1085–1996.

sky
sky

87. DAVID HOCKNEY (British, born 1937). **Photography is Dead. Long Live Painting. September 26th, 1995.**
Ink-jet print. 35 × 47 in (88.9 × 119.4 cm). Given by the Gordon Fraser Charitable Trust, 1997. E.516-1997.

88. Gabriel Orozco (Mexican, born 1962). **Breath on Piano (Aliento sobre piano)**, 1993. C-type colour photograph. 12½ × 18¾ in (31.8 × 47.7 cm). Bought 1997. E.517.1997.

pictures, now published and widely exhibited, 'working like therapy'. His most tender and subtle photograph shows his mother doing a jigsaw puzzle (Plate 86). Perhaps Billingham's photography was also a necessary distraction and maybe it put various psychological pieces together for him. His alert painter's eye saw a web of connexions in the scene, which his viewers, in their turn, become absorbed in matching and completing. His book *Ray's a Laugh* (1996) is the closest still photography has approached to the qualities we associate with the films of Mike Leigh: authenticity, complexity, and – as well as suspense – touching tenderness. As the photographer said to Robert Yates in the article already quoted: 'If people see the pictures and look down on my family, then they're not looking properly. I always thought that the photographs were moving'.

89. ADAM FUSS (British, born 1961). **Invocation**, 1992. 39½ × 29 in (99.6 × 72.3 cm). Dye destruction print. Bought from the photographer, 1993. E.693–1993.

Richard Billingham's puzzle picture recalls, and contrasts with, David Hockney's 'joiner' – or photo-collage – *Scrabble Game, Los Angeles, 1 January 1983*. The V&A was, through the Circulation Department, the first museum to buy and exhibit Hockney's now well known photographs (in 1971). The *Scrabble Game* was acquired and exhibited in 1983. It vividly demonstrates Hockney's 'joiner' method – and his critique of still photography.[13] Although Hockney has photographed constantly for his paintings and his personal albums, his 'joiners' – collages of hundreds of his photomat-printed snapshots – preoccupied him from 1982 to 1986. He returned to photography in 1995 in new circumstances. Among his recent works is one which he made in part as a get-well greeting for his friend Jonathan Silver, Director of the Hockney Gallery at Salts Mill, Bradford. Its title makes the piece particularly apposite to one of the themes of this book: *Photography is Dead. Long Live Painting. September 26th, 1995* (Plate 87). It was generously given to the Museum by the Gordon Fraser Charitable Trust. In 1995 Hockney made use of the latest technology to make this print. Nash Editions in Los Angeles had worked for some years on a new way to print photographs. They combined ink-jet technology with gouache pigment and fine paper – in this case, with Somerset heavyweight textured paper. Part of the pleasure of Hockney's picture lies in its variation on the artful games he has often played with different media representations, doubles and so on. Here he contrasts the photographed vase of sunflowers with the same vase and sunflowers painted in gouache on art paper. The composition was then photographed on colour transparency with a 10 × 8 in camera and printed in gouache on art paper by Nash Editions. Hockney's *jeu d'esprit* depended on photography, of course, for its execution.

Hockney's title probably refers, in part, to the transformation of photography by electronics. Apart from Helen Chadwick's *Viral Landscape* and Karen Knorr's *The New Justine*, already mentioned, the Museum has acquired other computer-edited photographs. *PHOTOGRAPHY NOW* included *Art of Memory*, a virtuoso 'electronic opera', by Woody Vasulka (which was later broadcast on British television), plus the

electronic composite portraits made by Nancy Burson with David Kramlich and Richard Carling. Other computer-edited photographs in the collection include works by Pedro Meyer and Alexa Wright, plus (in the National Art Library), the CD-ROM by Lewis Baltz, *The Deaths at Newport Beach* (1995).

Thanks to support from the Arts Council of England, the Photography Collection worked with the Arts Technology Workshop (ARTEC) in London to produce a CD-ROM on Camille Silvy's *River Scene, France* (1858). This was made for a touring exhibition on the photograph in 1995. It is not commercially available but can be viewed in the National Art Library. Digital technology was used to allow viewers to unveil the many layers of artifice in Silvy's photograph. Users may remove the sky (which Silvy had introduced, like Le Gray, from a separate negative), highlight his cunning retouching, take out the foreground 'burn-in' and finally remove the people Silvy had asked to pose. The CD-ROM demonstrates that photographic illusion relied on many kinds of subtle deception long before electronics gave the topic a new twist. The critical and theoretical literature of the past decades has also dispelled any illusions about the political 'neutrality' of photography. Thus, the authority of the photograph was in an advanced state of dissolution long before the electronic revolution arrived. Hence the emphasis by such dedicated documentarians as Lewis Baltz and Chris Killip on the fictional nature of their work, as we saw in the last chapter. The world of images may seem highly fictional – electronically composed, altered, tweaked – but it always was, as our excursion to the Rockies in chapter three may have suggested. Imagination is always involved.

Gabriel Orozco, a Mexican artist who is also based part-time in New York City, works in many media. He makes sculpture and installations as well as photographs. *Breath on Piano* (Plate 88) offers a different take on the still life. It might be considered a leisurely response to the title of Cartier-Bresson's most famous book, *Images à la Sauvette* ('At the Top of One's Breath') – or an installation of the most evanescent kind. Or not a still life at all, but a concise symbol of art and life.

Adam Fuss was born in London and lives in New York. Like many other artists of his generation – including Christopher Bucklow, Susan Derges and Garry Fabian Miller (all represented in the collection) – Fuss has returned to the simplest photographic means, to photography without the intervention of a camera.[14] The materials Fuss used to make *Invocation* (1992) (Plate 89) are simple: a sheet of positive colour paper in a tray of water, a baby and a flash. This is essentially the same procedure as Talbot used when he made the image of lace for *The Pencil of Nature* (Plate 1), or his friend Calvert Richard Jones with the leaf around 1845 (Plate 2). All they needed was an object and a sheet of sensitive paper. Adam Fuss used the same procedure, only by the 1990s the process had speeded up. Now both 'object' and paper are sensitive. This is not still life, but life itself. What better way to mark the millennium than with an image of a baby by a man named Adam?

Abbreviations and Notes

Abbreviations

AAD: Archive of Art and Design, V&A

NAL: National Art Library, V&A

Introduction

1. See Bernd Evers, ed., *Kunst in der Bibliotek*, Berlin: Kunstbibliotek, 1994.
2. Published by Abrams, Inc., New York, in association with the Baltimore Museum of Art.
3. The Victoria and Albert Museum: Publications and Exhibitions 1852–1996, London: Fitzroy Dearborn, 1997.

Chapter One: The New Art

1. Sir Henry Cole, *Fifty Years of Work of Henry Cole*, edited and completed by A.S. and H.L. Cole, London: G. Bell & Sons, 1884, p.3.
2. Elizabeth Bonython, *King Cole: A Picture Portrait of Sir Henry Cole, KCB 1808–1882*, London: V&A, 1982, p.4.
3. Janet Minihan, *The Nationalization of Culture: The Development of State Subsidies to the Arts in Britain*, London: Hamish Hamilton, 1977, p.41.
4. *Report from Select Committee [of the House of Commons] on Arts and Manufactures: together with The Minutes of Evidence, and Appendix*, London: Her Majesty's Stationery Office, 1835–6 pp.4–5.
5. Ibid., p.9.
6. Ibid., 1836, p.v.
7. W.H. Fox Talbot, *The Pencil of Nature*, part I, London: Longman, 1844–6, unpag.
8. Ibid., part I, unpag.
9. Derek R. Wood and Peter James, 'The Enigma of Monsieur de Sainte Croix', *History of Photography*, vol.17, no.1, Spring 1993, pp.101–14.
10. Ibid., p.106.
11. Richard Morris, 'More about de Ste Croix', *The PhotoHistorian*, no.106, January 1995, p.11.
12. Ibid.
13. Anon., 'A Claudet, F.R.S.: A Memoir', reprinted from *The Scientific Review*, for distribution at the meeting of the British Association at Norwich 19 August, London: Basil Montagu Pickering, 1868, pp.4–5.
14. Ibid.
15. Ibid, p.6.
16. W.H. Fox Talbot, op. cit., Plate XIII.
17. *The Athenaeum*, no.1008, 20 February 1847, p.185.
18. David Wooters, 'Daguerreotype Portraits by William E. Kilburn', *Image*, vol.33, nos 1 & 2, 1990, pp.21–9.
19. Derek R. Wood, 'The Daguerreotype in England; Some Primary Material Relating to Beard's Lawsuits', *History of Photography*, vol.3, no.4, 1979, p.306.
20. Rollin Buckman, *The Photographic Work of Calvert Richard Jones*, London: Her Majesty's Stationery Office [for the] Science Museum, 1990, p.29.
21. Eva White, *From the School of Design to the Department of Practical Art. The First Years of the National Art Library 1837–1853*, exhibition catalogue, V&A, London, 1994, p.3.
22. AAD, Ed.4/533: C.H. Wilson letter, 1 February 1847.
23. *Reports by the Juries, vol.II, Exhibition of the Works of Industry of All Nations*, London: Spicer Brothers, 1852, p.520.
24. Nancy Keeler, *History of Photography*. vol.6, no.3, July 1982, pp.257–72.
25. *Reports by the Juries*, op. cit., vol.II, p.521.
26. Ibid.
27. AAD.
28. Richard Redgrave, *An introductory address on the methods adopted by the Department of Practical Art to impart instruction to all classes of the community*, London: Her Majesty's Stationery Office, 1853, pp.80–1.
29. *Society of Arts Journal*, vol.XIV, no.794, 7 February 1868, p.236.
30. *The Photographic News*, vol.XII, no.490, 24 January 1868, p.38.

Chapter Two: 'A Vibrant Populist Enterprise'

1. Michael Conforti, 'The Idealist Enterprise and the Applied Arts', in *A Grand Design: The Art of the Victoria and Albert Museum*, exhibition catalogue, edited by Malcolm Baker and Brenda Richardson, Baltimore: The Baltimore Museum of Art, in association with the Victoria and Albert Museum, 1997.
2. Anthony Burton, forthcoming publication on the history of the V&A.
3. Conforti, op. cit.
4. Nadar, 'Quand j'étais photographe', in J.-F. Bory, *Nadar, t.2: Dessins et Ecrits*, Paris: A. Hubschmid, 1979, p.1187.
5. John Physick, *Photography and the South Kensington Museum*, London: Victoria and Albert Museum, 1975, p.1.
6. Mark Haworth-Booth, 'Henry Cole as Photographer', *The V&A Album*, Autumn 1988, London: De Montfort Publishing Ltd, 1988, pp.38–45.
7. NAL, Henry Cole, unpublished Diaries, 22 January 1856.
8. Elizabeth Anne McCauley, *'Industrial Madness': Commercial Photography in Paris 1848–1871*, New Haven and London: Yale University Press, 1994, pp.149–94.
9. *Journal of the Photographic Society*, vol.II, no.23, 21 October 1854, p.53.
10. *Journal of the Photographic Society*, vol.IV, no.58, 21 September 1857, p.46.
11. Mark Haworth-Booth, *Camille Silvy: 'River Scene, France'*, Getty Museum Studies on Art, Malibu: J. Paul Getty Museum, 1992, p.13.
12. Department of Science and Art, *Sixth Annual Report*, London: Her Majesty's Stationery Office, 1859, p.31.
13. W.A. Munford, *William Ewart MP 1798–1869: Portrait of a Radical*, London: Grafton & Co., 1960, p.177.
14. *Journal of the Photographic Society*, vol.V, no.71, 21 October 1858, p.37.
15. *Journal of the Photographic Society*, vol.IV, no.64, 22 March 1858, p.169.
16. Mark Haworth-Booth, *Camille Silvy*, op. cit.
17. Mark Haworth-Booth, 'The Dawning of an Age: Chauncy Hare Townshend, Eyewitness', in *The Golden Age of British Photography*, Philadelphia and New York: Philadelphia Museum of Art in association with Aperture, 1984, p.14.

18. *Journal of the Photographic Society*, vol.V, no.70, 21 September 1858, p.31.
19. Mark Haworth-Booth, 'Early Scottish Exhibitions', *History of Photography*, vol.18, no.3, Autumn 1994, pp.286–7.
20. *Journal of the Photographic Society*, vol.III, no.50, 21 January 1857, p.192.
21. Mark Haworth-Booth, 'The Dawning of an Age', op. cit., p.21.
22. V&A Registry, C.H. Townshend nominal file.
23. *Sixth Annual Report of the Science and Art Department*, London: Her Majesty's Stationery Office, 1859, p.36.

Chapter Three: All the World under the Subjugation of Art

1. Malcolm Baker, 'A Glory to the Museum: The Casting of the "Pórtico de la Gloria"', in *The V&A Album I*, London: Templegate Publishing Ltd in association with the Friends of the V&A, 1982, pp.101–08.
2. NAL, J.C. Robinson, unpublished Reports: 'List of Photographs to be made at Santiago by Mr Thompson', 3 September 1868.
3. Anthony Hamber, *'A Higher Branch of the Art': Photographing the Fine Arts in England, 1839–80*, Amsterdam: Gordon and Breach, 1996, p.303.
4. Ibid., p.427
5. Francis Haskell, *Rediscoveries in art — Some aspects of taste, fashion and collecting in England and France*, London: Phaidon, 1980, p.203, n.75.
6. Michael Conforti, 'The Idealist Enterprise and the Applied Arts', op. cit.
7. David Mattison, 'Arthur Vipond's Certificate of Competency in Photography', in *History of Photography*, vol.13, no.3, July–September 1989, pp.223–30.
8. Robert D. Monroe, 'The Earliest Pacific Northwest Indian Photograph 1860', in *Three Classic American Photographs: Texts and Contexts*, edited by G.M. Gidley, Exeter: American Arts Documentation Centre, University of Exeter, 1982, p.16.
9. Ibid., p.18.
10. Ibid., pp.18–19.
11. J.C.H. King, Department of Ethnography, British Museum, letter, 28 November 1996.
12. Joan Schwartz, 'The Photographic Record of Pre-Confederation British Columbia', *Archivaria*, no.5, 1977–8, pp.19–20.
13. Joanne Delzoppo, letter, 15 December 1996.
14. Janet Dewan, 'Photography for the Bombay and Madras Governments 1855–70', *History of Photography*, vol.16, no.4, Winter 1992, pp.302–17.
15. Ibid.
16. James Fergusson, *On the study of Indian architecture*, 2nd edn, London: John Murray, 1870, p.6.
17. Ibid., p.27.
18. *Society of Arts Journal*, vol.XVII, no.855, 9 April 1869, p.377.
19. Gary D. Sampson, 'The Success of Samuel Bourne in India', *History of Photography*, vol.16, no.4, Winter 1992, pp.338 and 346, note 32.
20. John Falconer and Satish Sharma, in *A Shifting Focus: Photography in India 1850–1900*, London: The British Council in association with the British Library, 1995.
21. Roland Barthes, *Camera Lucida*, London: Jonathan Cape, 1982, pp.38–40.
22. Lee Fontanella and Gerardo F. Kurtz, *Charles Clifford: fotografo de la España de Isabel II*, Madrid: Ediciones El Viso/Ministerio de Educacion y Cultura, 1996, p.185.
23. John Physick, *The Victoria and Albert Museum: The history of its building*, London: Victoria and Albert Museum, 1982, p.99.
24. F.H.W. Sheppard, *Survey of London*, vol. XXXVIII, London: The Athlone Press, 1975, chs 5 and 7.
25. V&A Registry, Alan S. Cole nominal file.

Chapter Four: A Fine Art and a Manufacturing Art

1. [Lady Eastlake], 'Photography' (unsigned article), *Quarterly Review*, vol.101, January–April 1857, p.444.
2. *Journal of the Photographic Society*, vol.II, no.24, 21 November 1854, p.59.
3. *House of Commons Select Committee on the South Kensington Museum*, London: Her Majesty's Stationery Office, 1860, p.78.
4. Mark Haworth-Booth, *Camille Silvy*, op. cit., pp.73–75.
5. Marina Warner, 'Parlour Made', *Creative Camera*, no.315, April/May 1992, pp.28–32.
6. V&A Registry, Guy Wilmot-Eardley nominal file.
7. *Photographic News*, vol.VII, no.234, 27 February 1863, p.99.
8. *The British Journal of Photography*, vol. X, no.203, 1 December 1863, p.466.
9. Steve Edwards, 'Photography, Allegory and Labor', *Art Journal*, Summer 1996, pp.38–44.
10. *Photographic News*, vol.VI, no.195, 30 May 1862, p.255.
11. *Photographic News*, vol.VI, no.192, 9 May 1862, p.223.
12. NAL, Henry Cole, unpublished Diaries, 19 May 1865.
13. NAL, Henry Cole, unpublished Correspondence, Box 8.
14. Charles and Frances Brookfield, *Mrs Brookfield and her Circle*, London: Sir Isaac Pitman and Sons, 1905, p.515.
15. *The Illustrated London News*, vol.XLVII, no.1339, 21 October 1865, p.383.
16. Mike Weaver, *Julia Margaret Cameron, 1815–1879*, London and Southampton: Herbert Press, 1984, p.15.
17. Ibid., p.26.
18. AAD, Presscuttings, Misc., Nov.1867–Feb 1868, p.1.
19. Sir Henry Cole, *Fifty Years of Work of Henry Cole*, op. cit., vol.II, p.347.
20. Paul Martin, *Victorian Snapshots*, London: Country Life, 1939, p.10.
21. Margaret Harker, 'Emerson and the Linked Ring', in Neil McWilliam and Veronica Sekules eds, *Life and Landscape: P.H. Emerson, Art & Photography in East Anglia 1885–1900*, Norwich: Sainsbury Centre for Visual Arts, 1986, p.66.
22. Margaret Harker, *The Linked Ring: the secession movement in photography in Britain, 1892–1910*, London: Heinemann, 1979, p.ix.
23. Ibid., pp.64–7.
24. Anne Kelsey Hammond, 'Aesthetic Aspects of the Photomechanical Print', in *British Photography in the Nineteenth Century: The Fine Art Tradition*, edited by Mike Weaver, Cambridge: Cambridge University Press, 1979, p.177.
25. *Report of the Board of Education*, London: Her Majesty's Stationery Office, 1899, p.68.
26. Horace Townsend, 'An Interview with Mr Frederick Hollyer', *The Studio*, vol.I, August 1893, pp.192–6.
27. Quoted by Margaret Harker, *The Linked Ring*, op. cit., pp.153–4.
28. *Photographic Journal*, vol.XXIV, 30 April 1900, pp.236–41.
29. *Second Report from the Select Committee on the Museums of the Science and Art Department, and Minutes of Evidence*, London: Her Majesty's Stationery Office, 1897.

Chapter Five: The Cosmopolitan Archive

1. AAD, Minutes of the Committee of Re-